# RENAL DIET
*Cookbook*
## for Beginners

*1500 Days of Low Sodium, Potassium and Phosphorus Easy and Delicious Recipes; Manage Chronic Kidney Disease and Avoid Dialysis with 28 Days Meal Plan*

Jessica T. Williams

© **Copyright 2022 by Jessica T. Williams- All rights reserved.**

This document is geared towards providing exact and reliable information in regard to the topic and issue covered.

- From a Declaration of Principles which was accepted and approved equally by a Committee of the American Bar Association and a Committee of Publishers and Associations.

In no way is it legal to reproduce, duplicate, or transmit any part of this document in either electronic means or in printed format. All rights reserved.

The information provided herein is stated to be truthful and consistent, in that any liability, in terms of inattention or otherwise, by any usage or abuse of any policies, processes, or directions contained within is the solitary and utter responsibility of the recipient reader. Under no circumstances will any legal responsibility or blame be held against the publisher for any reparation, damages, or monetary loss due to the information herein, either directly or indirectly.

Respective authors own all copyrights not held by the publisher.

The information herein is offered for informational purposes solely and is universal as so. The presentation of the information is without contract or any type of guarantee assurance.

The trademarks that are used are without any consent, and the publication of the trademark is without permission or backing by the trademark owner. All trademarks and brands within this book are for clarifying purposes only and are owned by the owners themselves, not affiliated with this document.

# Table of Contents

Introduction .................................................. 5
**Chapter 1: Basic introduction to the renal diet** .................................................. 6
**Chapter 2: What you Need to Know About Kidney Disease** .................................................. 11
**Chapter 3: The role of Sodium, Potassium and Phosphorus in the Body** .................................................. 16
**Chapter 4: Frequently Asked Questions** .... 18
**Chapter 5: Tips for success** .................................................. 21
**Chapter 6: Shopping list** .................................................. 23
**28 Day Meal Plan** .................................................. 26
**Breakfast Recipes** .................................................. 28
    Yogurt Bulgur .................................................. 28
    Strawberry Muesli .................................................. 28
    Goat Cheese Omelet .................................................. 29
    Chia Pudding .................................................. 29
    Rhubarb Muffins .................................................. 30
    Winter Fruit Salad .................................................. 30
    Mushroom Frittata .................................................. 31
    Buckwheat Granola .................................................. 31
    Breakfast Casserole .................................................. 32
    Egg Pockets .................................................. 32
    Breakfast Crepes .................................................. 33
    Italian Eggs with Peppers .................................................. 33
    Zucchini Fritters With Garlic Sauce .................................................. 34
    Winter Berry Smoothie .................................................. 34
    Zucchini and Egg Bowl .................................................. 35
    Kidney friendly Porridge .................................................. 35
    Veggie Mix of Mediterranean .................................................. 36
    Veggies Mix of Colors .................................................. 36
    Veggie Bowls .................................................. 37
    Chili Veggie and Quinoa Bowl .................................................. 37
    Swiss Chard Bowls .................................................. 38
    Rosemary Oats .................................................. 38
    Kale Smoothie .................................................. 39
    Millet Muffins .................................................. 39
    Apple Muesli .................................................. 40

**Lunch** .................................................. 41
    Grilled Duck Breast & Peach .................................................. 41
    Duck with Bok Choy .................................................. 41
    Turkey and Cauliflower Soup .................................................. 42
    Slow Cooker Turkey Legs .................................................. 42
    Chicken Leftovers Chowder .................................................. 43
    Lamb & Pineapple Kebabs .................................................. 43
    Stuffed Artichokes .................................................. 44
    Baked Meatballs & Scallions .................................................. 44
    Ginger Cauliflower Rice .................................................. 45
    Basil Zucchini Spaghetti .................................................. 45
    Cauliflower and Leeks .................................................. 46
    Braised Cabbage .................................................. 46
    Eggplant and Mushroom Sauté .................................................. 47
    Chicken Chili .................................................. 47
    Sausage & Egg Soup .................................................. 48
    Lamb Stew .................................................. 48
    Mint Zucchini .................................................. 49
    Celery and Kale Mix .................................................. 49
    Carrot Casserole .................................................. 50
    Kale, Mushrooms and Red Chard Mix ... 50
    Cauliflower Rice .................................................. 51
    Bok Choy And Beets .................................................. 51
    Pork with Pineapple .................................................. 52
    Pork with Bell Pepper .................................................. 52
    Spiced Pork .................................................. 53

**Dinner** .................................................. **54**
    Stuffed Zucchini Boats with Goat Cheese .................................................. 54
    Artichoke Matzo Mina .................................................. 54
    Creamy Penne .................................................. 55
    Greek Style Quesadillas .................................................. 55
    Light Paprika Moussaka .................................................. 56
    Mackerel Skillet with Greens .................................................. 56
    Dill Carrots .................................................. 57
    Zucchini Spaghetti .................................................. 57

Herbed Vegetable Trout ........................ 58
Citrus Glazed Salmon ......................... 58
Squash and Cranberries ...................... 59
Broiled Salmon Fillets ......................... 59
Spicy Sweet Potatoes ......................... 60
Salmon Balls with Cream Cheese .......... 60
Chili Mussels ..................................... 61
Fish Chili with Lentils .......................... 61
Fried Scallops in Heavy Cream ............ 62
Lettuce Seafood Wraps ...................... 62
Seafood Gratin .................................. 63
Mango Tilapia Fillets .......................... 63
Cabbage Beef Borscht ........................ 64
Lemon Pepper Beef Soup .................... 64
Jamaican Drumsticks .......................... 65
Cream of Crab Soup ........................... 65
Chicken with Asparagus ...................... 66

**Snacks and Desserts ........................ 67**
Baby Spinach and Dill Smoothie ........... 67
Avocado with Walnut Butter Smoothie .67
No-Bake Strawberry Cheesecake ......... 68
Blueberries and Coconut Smoothie ...... 68
Raw Lime, Avocado & Coconut Pie ..... 69
Blackberry & Apple Skillet Cake ........... 69
Black Forest Pudding .......................... 70
Pudding Muffins ................................. 70
Pineapple Sticks ................................. 71
Fried Pineapple Slices ......................... 71
Baked Apples .................................... 72
Grilled Peaches .................................. 72
Stuffed Apples ................................... 73
Rhubarb & Blueberry Granita .............. 73
Pumpkin Ice-Cream ............................ 74
Citrus Strawberry Granita ................... 74
Chocolaty Cherry Ice-Cream ............... 75
Collard Greens and Cucumber Smoothie ................................................. 75
Dark Turnip Greens Smoothie ............. 76
Creamy Dandelion Greens and Celery Smoothie .......................................... 76
Butter Pecan and Coconut Smoothie ..77
Fresh Cucumber, Kale and Raspberry Smoothie .......................................... 77
Banana Foster Pie .............................. 78
Almond Truffles ................................. 78
Fresh Lettuce and Cucumber-Lemon Smoothie .......................................... 79

**Conclusion .................................... 80**
**Index of Recipes ............................ 81**

# Introduction

Managing chronic kidney disease (CKD) requires lifestyle adjustments, but it might help to know you're not alone. In fact, over 31 million people in the United States are diagnosed with some malfunction of their kidneys or are battling kidney disease. Without knowing what the future holds, uncertainty, fear, depression, and anxiety can be common. It may even feel like dialysis is inevitable, and you may be asking yourself if it is worth the time or effort to try and manage this stage of the disease, or if it's even possible to delay the progression. So together, with the right tools, we can work to delay and ultimately prevent end-stage renal disease and dialysis. Success is earned through diet modifications and lifestyle changes. They have gone on to lead full, productive, and happy lives, continuing to work, play, and enjoy spending time with their loved ones—just the way it should be!

If making such changes seems difficult to you, then you can always ask for help from a loved one. You don't need to face all the challenges on your own, and this e-book is here to guide you through most of the aspects of the renal diet, but always ask for help or visit a doctor when you are in doubt about your health.

You can adopt the following tips in order to take care of yourself along with the specific diet:

Look carefully at labels when you buy over the counter medications. An excess of pain relief medications could lead to renal failure if you already have kidney disease or problems related to diabetes or high blood pressure. Especially in these cases, you should strictly follow your doctor's recommendations for managing your condition.

You should keep your alcohol intake low as well. Renal failure is more often than not, difficult to predict or even prevent. But you can certainly lower your risk of renal failure by taking good care of your kidneys. Here are the things that you can keep in mind for taking good care of your kidneys. Whenever you are buying any over the counter medication, you should pay close attention to the labels. You should always follow the directions that are given on these over-the-counter medicines like aspirin, ibuprofen and acetaminophen. Taking excess of the pain medication would increase the risk of renal failure and this is more likely when you already have any preexisting kidney disease or any other problem like diabetes or high blood pressure. You should work along with your doctor to manage your kidney problems. Keep yourself active, stay fit by exercising regularly and eat a balanced diet and consume alcohol in moderation, if you drink.

# Chapter 1: Basic introduction to the renal diet

Depending on the stage of your kidney disease, blood-work results, type of treatment and whether you have high blood pressure or diabetes, your renal diet "prescription" will vary.

In this section, we are going to discuss everything you need to know about the renal diet. We will also discuss important macronutrients, vitamins, and minerals, including:

- Potassium
- Phosphorus
- Calories
- Protein
- Fats
- Sodium
- Carbohydrates
- Vitamins/Minerals
- Fluids

## Potassium

Potassium is a crucial mineral that is required for the body to keep your heart strong and healthy. Healthy kidneys remove excess potassium through urination. However, when your kidneys are not working properly, they can't remove the potassium, so it builds up in the blood. Having too much or too little potassium in the blood can be dangerous to the body. Your potassium needs may vary depending on how well your kidneys are functioning. If you are receiving dialysis, you need to keep your potassium intake between 2,000 and 3,000 milligrams per day.

## Phosphorus

Healthy kidneys can remove extra phosphorus from the blood. However, when the kidneys are failing, phosphorus builds up into the blood and may cause problems. If you have chronic kidney disease or are receiving dialysis, phosphorous in the diet should be limited to between 800 and 1,000 milligrams per day.

## Calories

Your body needs more calories when you develop kidney disease, especially if you are on dialysis. In both chronic kidney disease and with dialysis, daily calorie requirements are 30 to 35 calories per kilogram of body weight. So, if your weight is 150 pounds, you need to consume 2,000 calories each day.

## Protein

If you are in stage 1,2, or 3 of chronic kidney disease, your protein intake will be limited to 12 to 15% of your calorie intake each day. If you are in stage 4 of chronic kidney disease, your protein intake will be reduced to 10% of your daily calorie intake. People who are on dialysis should eat about 1.2 grams of protein per kilogram of body weight each day. So, if you are 150 pounds, consume 82 grams of protein per day.

## Fats

If your doctor recommends you eat 2,000 calories, your calories from fat should be limited to 600 calories, it is about 70 grams of fat. You need to consume healthy fats such as olive oil, and fatty fish such as tuna and salmon.

## Sodium

When your kidneys do not work well, sodium starts to build up and can cause thirst, fluid-weight gain, and high blood pressure. You need to make some dietary modifications if you are in the early stages of chronic kidney disease. If you have stage 5 chronic kidney disease and require dialysis, then follow a low-sodium diet and do not consume more than 1,500 milligrams of sodium.

### Carbohydrates and fiber

Some carb-rich foods also contain fiber, and this plays an important role in improving your kidney disease condition. Fiber can help reduce kidney disease symptoms.

### Whole Grains

Whole grains in moderation can be very helpful for kidney disease patients.

Vitamin and Mineral Supplements

If you have kidney disease, then over-the-counter multivitamins are not good for your health. You need to avoid or limit vitamins A, E, and K because levels of these vitamins build up in the body as kidney function decreases. Talk with your physician about vitamin and mineral supplements.

### Fluids

Depending on your stage of kidney disease, you may need to limit the fluids you drink.

How to avoid "double trouble" foods

Double trouble foods – those that are high in both potassium and phosphorus including milk, and dairy foods, chocolate, nuts and seeds. These foods are best to avoid or use in small amounts.

## What is Renal Diet?

One of the most effective ways to prevent kidney disease is with proper diet.

It's also important to know that those who are at risk of this disease or have already been diagnosed with this condition can help alleviate symptoms and slow down the progression of the disease with a diet called the renal diet.

As you know, the wastes in the blood come from the foods and drinks that you consume.

When your kidneys are not functioning properly, they are unable to remove these wastes efficiently.

Wastes that remain in the blood can negatively affect your overall health.

Following a renal diet can help bolster the functioning of the kidney, reduce damage to the kidneys and prevent kidney failure.

So, what is a renal diet?

A renal diet is a type of diet that involves the consumption of foods and drinks that are low in potassium, sodium and phosphorus.

It also puts focus on the consumption of high-quality protein as well as limiting too much intake of fluids and calcium.

Since each person's body is different, it's important to come up with a specific diet formulated by a dietician to make sure that the diet is tailored to the needs of the patient.

Some of the substances that you have to check and monitor for proper renal diet include:

## The Benefits of Renal Diet

A renal diet minimizes the intake of sodium, potassium and phosphorus.

Excessive sodium is harmful to people who have been diagnosed with kidney disease as this causes fluid buildup, making it hard for the kidneys to eliminate sodium and fluid.

Improper functioning of the kidneys can also mean difficulty in removing excess potassium.

When there is too much potassium in the body, this can lead to a condition called hyperkalemia, which can also cause problems with the heart and blood vessels.

Kidneys that are not working efficiently find it difficult to remove excess phosphorus.

High levels of phosphorus excrete calcium from the bones causing them to weaken. This also causes elevation of calcium deposits in the eyes, heart, lungs, and blood vessels.

What to Eat and What to Avoid in Renal Diet

A renal diet focuses on foods that are natural and nutritious, but at the same time, are low in sodium, potassium and phosphorus.

## Foods for Renal Diet

Foods that you eat daily need to be regularly monitored. To encourage overall wellness, you need to take in less sodium, potassium, and phosphorus. Also, you need to eat more high-quality protein and lower your fluid uptake. Here is a detailed list of foods to eat and to avoid, which will make it easier for you to choose your next meal.

### High in Sodium Foods That You Need to Avoid

- Different meats and sausages: chicken, pork, and cuts that have been preserved, smoked, or cured
- Fishes and seafood that are preserved
- Frozen dinners or packed dinners
- Canned food items like pasta or soup
- Salted nuts
- Salted and canned beans
- Buttermilk
- Cheese, cheese products, processed cottage cheese
- Quick bread and bread with extra salt
- Salted rolls
- Biscuits and pancakes made by self-rising flour or their mixes
- Salted crackers
- The dough of pasta, potatoes, and rice that is processed and packaged
- Vegetables and vegetable juices in cans
- Salted regular pickles as well as olives and other pickled vegetables
- Vegetables made with pork products
- The dough of hash browns and scalloped potatoes, which are processed and packaged
- Quick pasta meals
- Processed ketchup
- Processed and salted mustard
- Processed salsa
- Dehydrated or regular soups in cans
- Processed or regular broths
- Cup noodles processed and salted ramen mixes
- Soy sauce
- Seasoning salts
- Marinades that are salted
- Salad dressings in bottles, processed or regular
- Salad dressings with bacon
- Salted butter and margarine
- Instant custard or pudding
- Ready-to-eat cakes

### Low in Sodium Foods That Should Be Taken Instead

- Fresh and frozen portions of lamb, poultry, beef, fish, shrimp, pork
- Fish and poultry, water and oil-packed, and drained; canned fish labeled as low sodium
- Eggs/egg substitutes
- Dried peas and not canned beans
- Low sodium peanut butter, almond, rice, or coconut milk, plant-based yogurts
- Low sodium cream cheese and low sodium cheeses like parmesan and ricotta
- Ready-to-eat cereals
- Rolls and bread that are not salted
- Almond, coconut, whole-wheat, low sodium plain and all-purpose white flour; low sodium corn and tortillas
- Low sodium breadsticks, crackers, unsalted popcorn, and chips
- Pasta and rice cooked without salt and low sodium noodles
- Frozen or fresh vegetables, low sodium canned vegetables without seasoning or sauce

- Low sodium vegetable juices, V-8, and low sodium tomato juice
- Low sodium pickles
- Fresh potatoes or unsalted and unseasoned frozen french fries and mashed potatoes
- Fresh and frozen canned fruits, dried fruits
- Low sodium salsa
- Low sodium soups that are canned
- Homemade broths made without any salt, and fresh ingredients
- Homemade pasta without any salt
- Low sodium soy sauce
- Low sodium seasoning and marinades
- Low sodium salad dressings
- Low sodium mayonnaise
- Unsalted butter and margarine, vegetable oils
- Homemade ketchup that is unsalted
- Unsalted mustard

## High in Potassium Foods That You Need to Avoid

- Cooked spinach, artichokes, okra, broccoli, beets, fried onions, and sweet potato
- Bananas, avocados, honeydew, mango, orange, pomegranate, prune, pumpkin, coconut, and cantaloupe
- Buttermilk and shakes
- Beans, either baked or refried
- Legumes, like lentils
- Nuts, like walnuts and raisins
- Granola
- Whole grains and bran
- Fast foods, like french fries and other salty foods
- Processed meats
- Vegetable juices
- Processed sauces, like tomato sauce
- Fruit juices such as pomegranate juice, prune juice
- Creamed soups
- Yogurt, frozen and regular
- Ice creams
- Chocolate sweet dishes

## Low in Potassium Foods That You Need to Eat Instead

- Asparagus, kale, broccoli, cucumber, zucchini, carrots, cabbage, bell pepper, eggplant, garlic, and lettuce
- Apples, grapes, pineapple, peaches, plum, all berries, watermelon
- Rice milk
- Greens beans and snow peas
- White rice and bread that is not whole
- Dried cranberries
- Unsalted popcorn
- Hash browns and mashed potatoes made up of leached potatoes
- Low sodium tomato and V-8 juice
- Unsalted sauces and apple sauce
- Unsalted noodles and pasta
- Non-dairy creams
- Sherbet
- Lemon and vanilla flavors instead of chocolate

## High in Phosphorus Foods That Need to Be Avoided

- Some Vegetables
- Some Fruits
- Parts of chicken and other poultry
- Ham and other pork products
- Hunted animals
- Some Seafood
- Plain Bread
- Tortillas
- Muffins
- Some pasta
- Some types of rice
- Certain cheeses
- Milk
- Yogurt

- Ice cream
- Eggs
- Snacks

### Low in Phosphorus Foods That Should Be Eaten Instead

- Celery, radishes, and baby carrots
- Apples, cherries, peaches, pineapples, blueberries, and strawberries
- Pot roast beef, sirloin steak
- Skinless chicken and turkey, breast and thighs
- Porkchop, mostly lean pork patty and pork roast
- Veal chop
- Wild salmon, mahi-mahi, king crab, lobster, snow crab, oyster shrimp, water, or oil-packed canned tuna
- Plain bread without salt, Italian bread, blueberry bread, sourdough bread, white bread, flatbread, wheat bread, pita bread, and cinnamon bread
- Flour tortillas, corn tortillas
- English muffins
- Macron, egg and rice noodles, spaghetti
- Couscous, long-grain white rice
- Cottage, blue, feta, parmesan, and cream cheese
- Almond, soy, and rice milk
- Non-dairy creamer
- Sorbet
- Pasteurized egg whites
- Unsalted popcorn

## Kidney-Friendly Protein Options Which Are Included in the Overall Diet

- Lean beef and turkey
- Meat substitutes, like tofu and veggie sausage
- Skinless chicken breast and thigh
- Salman, trout, mackerel fish, and shrimp
- Pork chops
- Cottage cheese
- Pasteurized eggs
- Greek yogurt
- Shakes made with rice, almond, coconut, or soy milk

## Kidney-Friendly Fluid Options Which Are Included in This Diet

- Fruits like apples, cherries, grapes, berries, peaches, plums
- Vegetables such as zucchini, cucumber, broccoli, cauliflower, cabbage, bell peppers, carrots, celery, lettuce, and eggplant
- Tea and coffee
- Gelatin
- Ice cubes
- Fruit juices
- Popsicles
- Milk substitutes
- Sherbet
- Low sodium soups

# Chapter 2: What you Need to Know About Kidney Disease

## Chronic Kidney Disease

Kidney disease is broken into two broad categories. Acute kidney injury, where sudden damage happens to the kidneys and chronic kidney disease, the gradual failure of the kidney's functions over a period of time. Acute kidney injury makes people more susceptible to chronic kidney disease and vice versa. Those who suffer from chronic kidney disease are more susceptible to acute kidney injuries. The best method of measuring the functionality of the kidneys is the glomerular filtration rate; this is also known as GFR.

The glomerular filtration rate is a way to figure out the functionality of the kidneys as well as calculate what state of kidney failure they are experiencing. GFR is a mathematical equation that uses the patient's race, age, gender, and serum creatinine level. Creatinine is waste products in the blood from muscle usage, and as kidney function decreases, the creatinine level in blood increases because filtration and excrement of waste in the blood are not being executed by the kidneys.

## Stages of CKD

There are five stages of CKD. Each level has a corresponding GFR index that accompanies it. It is very important for someone who has CKD to have continual monitoring of their GFR index because it doesn't take much for the change in the index to trigger the next stage of chronic kidney disease. For this reason alone, it is important to monitor what you are eating in conjunction with your stage of the disease.

### *Stage 1 and 2 CKD (Normal to High and Mild GFR)*

Most people who have stage one or two chronic kidney disease do not know that they have it. Their GFR index is generally greater than ninety milliliters per minute for stage one and an index that is sixty to eighty-nine milliliters per minute for stage two. Generally, the people who have been diagnosed with stage one or two CKD were diagnosed because of tests for another illness. Symptoms of stage one and two can be extremely vague, but a good indicator is higher than normal creatinine levels in the blood or urine. With stage two, the filtration levels of the kidney have begun to decrease, but not at an overly noticeable level. People living with stage one and two CKD can still live a normal life, they can't cure their kidneys, but they can help stop or slow the progression of the disease. Keeping blood pressure in line and eating a diet that is renal friendly are good first steps. Your doctor will keep up on your creatine levels and GFR to monitor the progression of CKD.

### *Stage 3A and 3B (Moderate GFR)*

Stage three is broken up into two GFR indexes, but the symptoms aren't much different. The GFR index for stage A is an index of forty-five to fifty-nine milliliters per minute. The GFR for stage B is thirty to forty-four milliliters per minute. As the kidney's functions decrease, the buildup of wastes causes the body to go into uremia, which is a buildup of that waste in the blood. More complications from kidney failure become apparent. The chances for high blood pressure increase and patients are likely to exhibit anemia. Swelling, or edema, may start to become apparent because of the water retention and typically starts in the arms and legs. Diet becomes increasingly more important with stage three CDK due to the buildup in the body.

### *Stage 4 (Severe GFR)*

Stage four is the last stop before kidney failure. The GFR index for stage four is fifteen to twenty-nine milliliters per minute. Stage four patients are more than likely receiving dialysis and are thinking about transplant in the near future. The body is barely filtering the wastes, hence the mechanical intervention for filtration, edema worsens, and physical symptoms can be overwhelming. Diet in this phase is stricter and will consist of limiting things that can build up in the body that the kidneys are no longer taking care of on their own.

### Stage 5 (End Stage GFR)

Once the kidneys are no longer filtering the waste in the body, dialysis will be necessary to live. The GFR index in the end-stage is less than fifteen milliliters per minute. There is also a chance that if you meet qualifications, you will be put on a transplant list. Stage five CKD leaves the patient feeling sick almost all of the time because of the toxins and waste built up in the body. A nephrologist, a doctor who specializes in kidneys, will be a permanent part of your medical regimen. Diet will be an absolute must, as will limiting fluid intake.

## Renal disease diagnostic tests

Besides identifying the symptoms of kidney disease, there are other better and more accurate ways to confirm the extent of loss of renal function. There are mainly two important diagnostic tests:

### Urine test

The urine test clearly states all the renal problems. The urine is the waste product of the kidney. When there is a loss of filtration or any hindrance to the kidneys, the urine sample will indicate it through the number of excretory products present in it. The severe stages of chronic disease show some amount of protein and blood in the urine. Do not rely on self-tests; visit an authentic clinic for these tests.

### Blood pressure and blood test

Another good way to check for renal disease is to test the blood and its composition. A high amount of creatinine and other waste products in the blood clearly indicates that the kidneys are not functioning properly. Blood pressure can also be indicative of renal disease. When the water balance in the body is disturbed, it may cause high blood pressure. Hypertension can both be the cause and symptom of kidney disease and therefore should be taken seriously.

## How to keep your kidneys healthy

Like all other parts of the body, human kidneys also need much care and attention to work effectively. It takes a few simple and consistent measures to keep them healthy. Remember that no medicine can guarantee good health, but only a better lifestyle can do so. Here are a few of the practices that can keep your kidneys stay healthy for life.

### Active lifestyle

An active routine is imperative for good health. This may include regular exercise, yoga, or sports and physical activities. The more you move your body, the better its metabolism gets. The loss of water is compensated by drinking more water, and that constantly drains all the toxins and waste from the kidneys. It also helps in controlling blood pressure, cholesterol levels, and diabetes, which indirectly prevents kidney disease.

### Control blood pressure

Constant high blood pressure may cause glomerular damage. It is one of the leading causes, and every 3 out of 5 people suffering from hypertension also suffer from kidney problems. The normal human blood pressure is below 120/80 mmHg. When there is a constant increase of this pressure up to 140/100mmHg or more it should be immediately put under control. This can be done by minimizing the salt intake, controlling the cholesterol level and taking care of cardiac health.

### Hydration

Drinking more water and salt-free fluids proves to be the life support for kidneys. Water and fluids dilute the blood consistency and lead to more urination; this in turn will release most of the excretions out of the body without much difficulty. Drinking at least eight glasses of water in a day is essential. It is basically the lack of water that strains the kidneys and often hinders the glomerular filtration. Water is the best option, but fresh fruit juices with no salt and preservatives are also vital for kidney health. Keep all of them in constant daily use.

## Dietary changes

There are certain food items which taken in excess can cause renal problems. In this regard, an extremely high protein diet, food rich in sodium, potassium, and phosphorous can be harmful. People who are suffering from early stages of renal disease should reduce their intake, whereas those facing critical stages of CKD should avoid their use altogether. A well-planned renal diet can prove to be significant in this regard. It effectively restricts all such food items from the diet and promotes the use of more fluids, water, organic fruits, and a low protein meal plan.

## No smoking/alcohol

Smoking and excessive use of alcohol are other names for intoxication. Intoxication is another major cause of kidney disease, or at least it aggravates the condition. Smoking and drinking alcohol indirectly pollute the blood and body tissues, which leads to progressive kidney damage. Begin by gradually reducing alcohol consumption and smoking down to a minimum.

## Monitor the changes

Since the early signs of kidney disease are hardly detectable, it is important to keep track of the changes you witness in your body. Even the frequency of urination and loss of appetite are good enough reasons to be cautious and concerning. It is true that only a health expert can accurately diagnose the disease, but personal care and attention to minor changes are of key importance when it comes to CKD.

## Prevent or manage conditions that increase the risk for kidney disease

The most important thing that you can do in avoiding kidney disease is to prevent the health conditions that cause harm to your kidneys. Type 2 diabetes and high blood pressure were mentioned to be the culprits for most cases of kidney disease. Prevention of these conditions is the best way to avoid becoming part of that statistic.

If you already have any of the conditions mentioned that cause kidney disease, it is best to talk with your doctor on how you can prevent it. It would also be best to follow the next suggestions in this part of the book.

## Hydrate well

Drinking enough water is vital for your kidney health. Having not enough fluids causes your kidney to produce urine with a higher concentration of the minerals and waste that it filters from your blood. This increases the risk of kidney stone formation.

It is recommended to drink at least ten 200-milliliter glasses spread throughout the day. It should be noted that those with an existing kidney condition should monitor how much fluid they drink.

## Monitor and moderate intake of over-the-counter medicines

Some over-the-counter medicines can cause damage to your kidneys if taken for long periods of time. Some can even cause acute kidney injury if you take them while not properly hydrated. This is why you have to be cautious with what you take and always ask your pharmacist if what you are buying can affect your kidneys. OTC medications that you should watch out for include nonsteroidal inflammatory drugs like ibuprofen and naproxen.

## Reduce stress

High levels of stress cause your body to have a higher blood pressure, faster heart rate, and elevated levels of blood sugar and cholesterol. These can eventually lead to type-2 diabetes or cardiovascular disease that will damage your kidneys.

You can manage your stress levels by adopting relaxation techniques and by having adequate sleep and relaxation. You can also help your body cope with stress by exercising regularly, having a healthy diet, and having a positive mental attitude and outlook in life.

### *Make healthy food choices*

You would want a diet that decreases the risk of the diseases that contribute to kidney disease. The foods you should watch out for are those that are high in added sugar, artificial sweeteners, sodium, and fat. Examples of these items include soda, processed foods, pre-made or microwave meals, canned goods, and junk food.

Instead, choose healthier alternatives that you can easily find in the grocery. Enrich your diet with lean cuts of meat, and fresh fruits and vegetables. You can also use a variety of herbs and spices available to cook your food instead of relying on salt. Lastly, you can replace simple carbohydrates in your diet with whole carbohydrates like brown rice, whole wheat, oats, and other whole grains.

## How to Avoid Dialysis

The key to avoiding dialysis is to stop the progression of dialysis. This can be done given that you can take the necessary measures as early as the first or second stage of kidney disease. It is best to stop smoking, moderate the use of nonsteroidal medication, start exercising daily, maintain a healthy weight, and start a healthier diet and lifestyle. If the kidney disease is brought about by high blood pressure or type-2 diabetes, treating and managing these conditions will help in halting its progress.

It is also recommended to work closely with a nephrologist and a dietitian in treating and managing the health of your kidneys. They can determine what is best for your current health and the current state of your kidneys. A personalized treatment plan would always be the best way to stop the progression of this disease. These medical professionals will take into account every aspect of your health, which is even more important if your kidney disease is brought about by type-2 diabetes or high blood pressure.

## Key recommendations

Chronic kidney disease is a slow-progressing disease and does not cause the patient a lot of complaints in the initial stages. The group of diseases referred to as chronic kidney disease includes several kidney diseases in which the renal function decreases for several years or decades. If you have been diagnosed with chronic kidney disease, your lifestyle and diet may need to change to keep your kidney functioning at the proper level. You can do a lot to help with the treatment.

Regularly visit the doctor and be sure to do the tests with the frequency as prescribed by the doctor. Know the value of your main indicators - glomerular filtration rate (GFR) and serum creatinine level.

Strictly monitor the treatment plan and discuss with the doctor or nurse all questions and problems arising from the disease and its treatment.

Use only those drugs that have been prescribed and approved by a doctor. Some medicines can damage kidneys. Know the names of the drugs and their doses. Take them only as prescribed by your doctor.

Use only those nutritional supplements and vitamins that your doctor recommended.

When visiting doctors, always inform them that you have chronic kidney disease. You must also inform your doctor that another doctor has prescribed a course of treatment for you if there is any.

If you need to do examinations with a contrast agent (for example, computed tomography, angiography, magnetic resonance imaging), then discuss them first with your doctor and follow his directions.

If you have high blood pressure, you should know the recommended level of blood pressure and keep it under control. It is essential to protect the kidneys.

If you have diabetes, monitor your blood sugar levels, stick to your prescribed diet, and take your medicine.

Know your cholesterol level. When your cholesterol level increased, carefully monitor your recommended lifestyle. It is crucial to maintain a diet, an active lifestyle, weight maintenance at a level that is normal for you to monitor your cholesterol level.

Observe a healthy diet. If you need to limit the intake of any product, plan the composition of your meal so that you can get from it all the necessary nutrients and calories.

If you are overweight, try to find safe methods of losing weight with your doctor. Losing bodyweight will help the kidneys to work longer in normal mode.

Do not skip meals or stay without food for several hours.

Try to eat 4-5 small amounts of food instead of 1-2 main meals.

Drink enough fluids. If your doctor has prescribed for you limited fluid intake, then it is essential to follow this recommendation. If you are still tormented by thirst, you can quench it by putting a slice of lemon in your mouth or rinsing your mouth with water.

Reduce the amount of salt consumed with food.

Be physically active. Physical activity helps to reduce blood pressure, blood sugar, and cholesterol levels, and also helps you to better cope with the disease.

If you smoke, find an opportunity to quit this habit.

Try to be active in the process of maintaining your health.

Search and find information about chronic kidney disease and its treatment.

If you have diabetes, monitor your blood sugar levels, stick to your prescribed diet, and take your medicine.

Know your cholesterol level. When you increase your cholesterol level, carefully monitor your recommended lifestyle. To do this, it is very important to maintain a diet, an active lifestyle, weight maintenance at a level that is normal for you, and medication.

Observe a healthy diet. If you need to limit the intake of any product, plan the composition of your meal so that you can get from it all the necessary nutrients and calories.

If you are overweight, try to find safe methods of losing weight with your doctor. Losing body weight will help the kidneys to work longer in normal mode.

Do not skip meals or stay without food for several hours.

Try to eat 4-5 small amounts of food instead of 1-2 main meals.

Drink enough fluids. If your doctor has prescribed for you limited fluid intake, then it is essential to follow this recommendation. If you are still tormented by thirst, you can quench it by putting a slice of lemon in your mouth or rinsing your mouth with water.

Reduce the amount of salt consumed with food.

Be physically active. Physical activity helps to reduce blood pressure, blood sugar, and cholesterol levels, and also helps you to better cope with the disease.

If you smoke, find an opportunity to quit this habit.

Try to be active in the process of maintaining your health.

Search and find information about chronic kidney disease and its treatment.

# Chapter 3: The role of Sodium, Potassium and Phosphorus in the Body

## The Role of Sodium in the Body

Sodium is considered the most important electrolyte of the body next to chloride and potassium. The electrolytes are actually the substance that controls the flow of fluids into the cells and out of them. Sodium is mainly responsible for regulating blood volume and pressure. It is also involved in controlling muscle contraction and nerve functions. The acid-base balance in the blood and other body fluids is also regulated by sodium. Though sodium is important for the health and regulation of important body mechanisms, excessive sodium intake, especially when a person suffers from some stages of chronic kidney disease, can be dangerous. Excess sodium disrupts the critical fluid balance in the body and inside the kidneys. It then leads to high blood pressure, which in turn negatively affects the kidneys. Salt is one of the major sources of sodium in our diet, and it is strictly forbidden on the renal diet. High sodium intake can also lead to Edema, which is swelling of the face, hands, and legs. Furthermore, high blood pressure can stress the heart and cause the weakening of its muscles. The build-up of fluid in the lungs also leads to shortness of breath.

Sodium is one of the elements necessary for the proper functioning of the body. He is primarily responsible for water and electrolyte management, but also has other functions. What are his other roles? Are there severe effects of excess and deficiency of sodium? How to introduce a diet that will allow us to reduce sodium intake?

Sodium has important functions in the body, and disturbances in its concentration can cause serious problems. The main tasks of this valuable element include:

Maintaining the osmotic balance of the body in the extracellular fluids of the body - this means that it regulates the volume of water in the body and protects us from dehydration,

Maintaining acid-base balance (together with potassium and chlorine),

Involved in the conduction of nerve impulses - sodium is a potassium antagonist, and this element creates a concentration difference on both sides of the cell membrane, thus enabling the transmission of impulses. This process is responsible for the state of smooth muscle, skeletal and heart tension,

Participation in the process of glucose and amino acid transport across cell membranes,

Activating salivary amylase - a digestive enzyme present in saliva.

Normal sodium concentration in the body is 135-145 mmol /l, and its maintenance is responsible for the renin-angiotensin-aldosterone system. It is a complex hormonal-enzyme system that also regulates the volume of water in the body.

## Potassium - role in the body

Potassium is another mineral that is closely linked to renal health. Potassium is another important electrolyte, so it maintains the fluid balance in the body and its pH levels as well. This electrolyte also plays an important role in controlling nerve impulses and muscular activity. It works in conjugation with the sodium to carry out all these functions. The normal potassium level in the blood must range between 3.5 and 5.5mEq/L. It is the kidneys that help maintain this balance, but without their proper function, the potassium starts to build up in the blood. Hyperkalemia is a condition characterized by high potassium levels. It usually occurs in people with chronic kidney disease. The prominent symptoms of high potassium are numbness, slow pulse rate, weakness, and nausea. Potassium is present in green vegetables and some fruits, and these ingredients should be avoided on a renal diet.

Potassium belongs to microelements and is an element that performs many essential functions. Thanks to potassium, our cells can transmit electrical impulses, but potassium also helps maintain adequate blood pressure and muscle tone.

Potassium, therefore, is an electrolyte, controls muscle function. It enables the generation of electrical impulses in the cells of our body, including in the cells of the heart muscles, i.e., it is responsible for each heartbeat. Potassium plays the same function in skeletal muscles.

Potassium is involved in the processes in which our cells synthesize proteins, which in turn are muscle building blocks. Thus, potassium is one of the factors that control muscle building and help maintain healthy muscle mass.

Potassium, being also a calcium antagonist, is responsible for proper muscle tone (so-called tonus) by raising their tone.

Also, potassium helps maintain acid-base balance, and thus maintain the homeostasis of the whole body.

If our body is functioning properly, balance is maintained between potassium and sodium. Disorders in the concentrations of these macro-elements cause the occurrence of one of the most common and severe civilization diseases, i.e., hypertension and heart disease. Unlike sodium, low potassium levels promote these diseases.

People rarely suffer from potassium deficiency or bearing. This happens, however, in cases where the functioning of our body is disturbed.

Potassium deficiency, or hypokalemia, can occur when we use high blood pressure diuretics, in the case of prolonged vomiting or diarrhea, and with some kidney problems. Symptoms of hypokalemia are weak, flaccid muscles, arrhythmias, and a slight increase in blood pressure.

Hyperkalemia, which is too high in potassium, causes a dangerous arrhythmia. Hyperkalemia occurs when the kidneys are weak, infections are severe, and when you are taking some heart medicines.

## The role of Phosphorus in the body

The amount of phosphorus in the blood is largely linked to the functioning of the kidneys. Phosphorus, in combination with vitamin D, calcium, and parathyroid hormone, can regulate the renal function. The balance of phosphorous and calcium is maintained by the kidneys, and this balance keeps the bones and teeth healthy. Phosphorous, along with vitamin D, ensures the absorption of calcium into the bones and teeth, where this mineral is important for the body. On the other hand, it gets dangerous when the kidneys fail to control the amount of phosphorus in the blood. This may lead to heart and bone-related problems. Mainly there is a high risk of weakening of the bones followed by the hardening of the tissues due to the deposition of phosphorous and calcium outside the bones. This abnormal calcification can occur in the lungs, skin, joints, and arteries, which can become in time very painful. It may also result in bone pain and itching.

Because as much as 85% of phosphorus is found in bones and teeth, it is necessary to maintain their proper structure. It also occurs in soft tissues and cell membranes, i.e., in the tissues of muscles, heart, and brain. It also plays an essential role in the process of growth and reconstruction or repair of damaged tissues. As one of the elements that take part in the processes occurring in the human body, phosphorus is also an energy transmitter. Thanks to this mineral, food is converted into energy that translates into muscle work.

Phosphorus also ensures the proper functioning of nerves and the brain and is involved in many chemical reactions and metabolic processes in our body. It maintains the overall vitality of the body. Also, it plays an important role in the work of the heart. For researchers, it is an essential carrier of genetic information because it is a component of DNA.

# Chapter 4: Frequently Asked Questions

Adapting to a new diet is a journey that brings about a lot of discoveries and questions about additional changes and options. The Renal Diet is no exception, and while it can be modified to suit custom preferences and tastes, you may have questions about the choices you make and how different foods and drinks affect your kidneys' health.

**Question: Is a plant-based diet required to maximize the benefits of a renal diet?**

Answer: A vegan diet is not a requirement of the renal diet, though it can be a great benefit if this is your preference. The most important aspect of eating well is to focus on fresh, plant-based foods, as they are easy to digest and contain significant amounts of nutrients. If you choose lean meats as part of your meal plan, be sure to include as many fresh fruits and vegetables as possible and limit the portions of animal protein with each serving, while increasing the amount of fiber and other nutrients.

**Question: What happens if I find out that a specific food in my diet is too high in sodium, phosphorus, potassium or protein? Do I have to eliminate it completely, or may I indulge on occasion?**

Answer: If your condition is severe, you may want to consult with a doctor or specialist before making a firm decision. For most people, the occasional food choice – such as a banana, which is high in potassium – is not going to have a negative impact and is often offset with many other health benefits within the renal diet guidelines, if followed closely. For this reason, there should be no adverse effects on your kidneys or health overall. In some cases, a dietitian or doctor may recommend certain foods outside of the renal diet if they notice a significant improvement in your kidneys and/or to treat another ailment that could be related to kidney issues, such as high blood pressure or diabetes.

**Question: What happens if I eat too much of the wrong foods and get off track. Is it too late to start the diet over again?**

Answer: While it's important to adhere to this diet as much as possible – especially in more severe cases where renal function is low – don't get distracted by making the wrong food choices by switching back immediately. The odd "slip up" is expected, and anyone can make this error from time to time. It's most important to keep the basis of your food choices with your kidneys in mind, to avoid future errors and move towards a healthier lifestyle.

**Question: Can I drink the occasional soda on the renal diet? Is it acceptable if the soda is sugar-free?**

Answer: Drinking soda of any kind should be avoided, as the sugar content is so high (almost 30 grams of sugar in one can!). Artificial sweeteners in sugar-free sodas tend to be unhealthy and may cause unpleasant side effects of their own. If you want to enjoy a carbonated beverage, choose sparkling water with low sodium. Some of these drinks offer natural flavoring with little or no sugar, which makes them an excellent substitute.

**Question: Is there a short list of foods to avoid?**

Answer: Initially, when you begin this diet, it can be challenging to determine which foods are best to avoid. Unfortunately, while there is no short list, knowing which foods and types of meals to stay away from becomes easier in time. One of the first steps you can take is to avoid salty foods, which are known to be high in sodium and not a good fit for the renal diet. Foods high in protein should be limited as well, especially red meats. Plant-based sources of protein are much better for digestion, and easier on the kidneys. Foods high in phosphorus and potassium will become common once you familiarize yourself with them. In general, a better way to approach this diet is to focus on the foods you can have, as opposed to those you must limit or avoid.

**Question: I've been following the renal diet for several months, but there haven't been any significant improvements to my kidneys. Does the renal diet work for everyone, or just some people?**

Answer: The answer to this question can vary dramatically, depending on the severity of the disease and the stage of renal failure. In extreme cases where dialysis is involved, dietary changes may take much longer to have an impact than in situations where kidney disease has not progressed past the early stages and remains relatively easy to manage with diet. Other factors that may impact the variance in success or kidney improvement include the amount of excess weight, as it can take longer for some people to lose extra weight than others, glucose levels, and various stages of heart disease and/or type 2 diabetes. Given the number of variables that may affect your progress on the renal diet, always allow more time and keep a diary or journal to track any changes you notice. It may take longer than you expect, but by consistently following the meal plans and making better choices, you'll definitely see changes.

**Question: How do I know if I'm eating too much protein or sodium? How can I avoid eating more phosphorus or potassium than my kidneys can handle, and when do I know when I've had too much?**

Answer: Keeping a journal of your food options for meal planning is an ideal way to review your diet. Stay in regular contact with your doctor and share your meal plans, so they know exactly what you are eating on a daily basis. It may seem like a lot of work, but it's worthwhile until you become used to making informed decisions about the foods you eat. Every individual's circumstance is different: some people may have more leniency with the volume of protein and potassium they can consume, while those who use dialysis may need to restrict their choices further, to ensure they can get the most out of the renal diet plan.

**Question: Does the renal diet guarantee healthy kidneys if it is used as a preventative diet?**

Answer: There is no guarantee that your kidneys will always function the same, and this refers to both healthy and impaired organs. Most people don't pay attention to the health of their kidneys until they are diagnosed with a condition, and only then are they faced with the decision to make dietary changes as soon as possible. Taking preventative measures doesn't necessarily require adherence to the renal diet, though aspects of this way of eating can be implemented into your diet to better support your kidneys while they are working well. If you have a family or friends with kidney conditions, eating a renal-cautious diet with them and sharing meals is a good way to show your support while helping yourself at the same time.

The best prevention is eating natural, whole foods, and focusing more on plant-based sources of nutrients. Reduce your animal proteins, and ensure you get the nutrients you need in moderation, without consuming too much sodium or protein. There is never a full guarantee that eating a well-balanced diet will prevent kidney disease completely, though it can be a great defense against renal disease and failure.

**Question: Can the renal diet heal kidneys completely and restore their function before they became infected?**

Answer: Once damage to the kidneys occurs, it cannot be reversed – however, improvements can be made to ensure further damage is prevented and better function is restored, at least to an extent. For people who suffer from more advanced stages of renal disease, it is most important that the progress of the condition is arrested, so they can live longer and experience a better-quality life. Adhering to a renal diet is one way to ensure the kidneys get a "break" from toxins. Once you reach the stage of dialysis, it is vital to choose your meals as carefully as possible, as this becomes a requirement for the remainder of your life. If dietary and lifestyle changes can be successfully made prior to this stage, the prognosis is excellent, and you can lead a normal, productive life. Now more than ever, as we learn about the importance of kidney health, management of renal disease becomes a chronic condition with fewer complications, as long as you live a healthy lifestyle.

**Question: Can medications interfere with the renal diet plan?**

Answer: When prescribed a medication, either for your kidneys or another condition, always take the time to read about possible side effects, including food items to avoid. This may include some foods recommended on the renal diet. If in doubt, avoid any specific foods you may encounter reactions with as a result of the medication, and consult with a pharmacist or doctor before proceeding. It's always best to avoid potential complications and play it safe before combining a potentially dangerous mix.

**Question: Is kidney failure hereditary?**

Answer: While there are some predisposed conditions that could lead to a higher chance of kidney disease or infection, there is no evidence to suggest kidney disease or renal failure is, in itself, hereditary.

It is a fully preventable condition, and if you know of any kidney disease history in your family, you may be more likely to pay attention to the warning signs, especially early symptoms. Choosing your foods carefully and avoiding overeating and consuming processed foods will help you prevent kidney problems later in life.

**Question: There are so many things I can't eat now—what can I eat?**

A: What you should eat and how much is determined by what stage of CKD you are in. Routine checkups and lab work will help determine your food restrictions. This book is a guide that focuses on kidney-supportive foods—and the list is a long one! However, a registered dietitian (RD) can also help you sort out what foods to avoid and, more importantly, what foods you can have. An RD can help you develop personalized diet parameters and create practical individualized meal plans and lists of foods to meet your dietary needs to supplement those discussed in this book. A good RD can answer your questions and empower you to make your own smart and satisfying food choices.

**Question: Is there a cure for CKD?**

There is no cure for CKD. However, there are many ways to manage the disease and live a long, full, productive life. If you have CKD, it is very important to have regular checkups, take your medication as prescribed, and follow your CKD diet/meal plan to slow the progression of the disease. The one thing you have complete control over is the choice of what and how much you eat. Diet compliance is one of the most important components of your health, as it influences your future health and well-being.

**Question: What can cause CKD?**

Over time, other chronic diseases, such as diabetes, hypertension, or heart disease, can cause CKD. It can also be genetic or linked to ethnicities such as Native American, Hispanic, African American, or Asian. Age is another factor; people over 60 years old are at a higher risk for CKD.

**Question: Can I exercise if I have CKD?**

Absolutely! Exercising at least 30 minutes, five days a week, can help keep symptoms in check and control associated factors, such as diabetes and hypertension.

What is a glomerular filtration rate (GFR) and why do I keep seeing numbers associated with this term?

The GFR is used to measure how well your kidneys are functioning. This number is used along with the amount of creatinine in your blood to calculate what stage of CKD you may be in, so it is important to talk to your doctor about these tests.

**Question: How can I tell if my CKD is getting worse?**

Many symptoms are not noticeable until the advanced stages of CKD. It is important to begin adopting a kidney-friendly diet and lifestyle before your condition worsens. Regular checkups are helpful and reassuring, as your provider can monitor your levels and answer your questions. If you notice symptoms such as swelling, constant fatigue, changes in appetite, foamy urine, or trouble with concentration, please contact your doctor.

**Question: If I have CKD, am I going to need dialysis?**

CKD, especially if caught early, can be controlled, and advanced stages can be delayed with proper nutrition and lifestyle changes. In fact, only about 1 out of 50 people who are diagnosed with CKD progress to kidney failure and the need for dialysis. CKD does result in a higher risk for other complications, such as heart disease or stroke; this is one more good reason to work with your doctor and dietitian to manage your diet and medications and prevent any further damage.

# Chapter 5: Tips for success

## Maintain Your Blood Sugar in the Target Range

When you are checking blood sugar levels, you might find out that your blood sugar levels go through quite a few changes. It is not important to focus on these changes heavily when gauging the blood sugar levels, but they are important to know if you would like to get more details of your sugar levels. Before venturing further into understanding your glucose levels, I would like to first draw your attention to a particular measurement – mmol/L.

'Mmol' is short for millimole. A mole essentially calculates just how many atoms of a particular mineral or compound is present in a chemical process or reaction. A millimole is one-thousandth of a mole. The measurement is used to make precise calculations of the contents of fluids in our body, especially when it comes to blood sugar levels. The 'L' in mmol/L represent liters. What the measurement is trying to show you is the number of atoms of glucose or sugar (represented in mmol) is present in every liter of your blood. A typical adult will have anywhere between 4.7 to 5.5 liters of blood in their body. By using mmol/L, you get to know if you have high or low sugar content.

## Maintain Your Blood Pressure in the Target Range

You must have guessed that this tip was coming. Well, here it is and it goes side-by-side with the previous tip. Once again, before we dive headfirst into the tip itself, it is time to understand the measurement used to indicate blood pressure levels - mmHg.

When measuring the pressure levels in your blood, one cannot simply say that you have a certain level of pressure. That is because the pressure is a difficult concept to explain. It is similar to asking a person to measure the levels of pain he or she feels from various injuries. In order to make it easier to understand blood pressure, it gets compared to a column of mercury. The 'mm' in mmHg stands for millimeters and Hg is the chemical symbol for mercury. Each unit of the measurement explains how much pressure a column of mercury 1 millimeter high exerts. For example, if the reading shows 2 mmHg, then the pressure exerted by your blood is similar to the pressure exerted by a column of mercury 2 millimeter high. Now you can, more or less, imagine how pressure works in the blood. You have a reference point – which is mercury in this case – to work with.

An ideal blood pressure level is when the readings are below 120/80 mmHg. If the blood pressure falls between 120/80mmHg to 139/89mmHg, then the pressure falls in the normal to high range. Blood pressure over the 140/90mmHg mark is considered as high.

Here is the truth; even if you have had low blood pressure all your life, you might find it difficult to manage your blood pressure after having CKD. The diet will definitely go a long way in blood pressure management, but you should still get in touch with your doctor to see if you might need medicines to further keep the pressure in check. Try to check your pressure every day so that you are on top of things and are ready to take action at the first sign of an above-normal result.

## Maintain Your Weight

When the body has extra weight, all of that weight gets pushed downwards. It makes the kidneys work much harder and filter wastes that are more than the regular level. All of the extra work only adds more burden on the kidneys and eventually, you begin to see the results. Remember this, your kidney has more work to deal with.

At this point, it is important to mention this; being overweight is nothing to be ashamed about. Rather, it gives you a starting point for your goals and helps you decide where you would like to go next. It tells you just how much physical activity you must incorporate into your life in order to start noticing visible changes. Sure, the road to a healthy body is filled with numerous obstacles, some of which are challenging to overcome. But the rewards are worth it. You are not looking to get the "ideal body," "perfect body" or the "six-pack abs." You are trying to get your body to a state where it results in positive effects on your health.

## Quit Smoking and Sodas

Sodas are packed with more sugar than your kidneys can handle. In fact, you might just be pushing your kidneys to overwork in order to properly filter through all that sugar. This is why it comes as no surprise that when you have CKD, you should aim to manage the sugar content you consume, not just from sodas, but from other sweet and sugar-filled substances.

If you had been smoking, now would be a good time to get rid of the habit. Don't think of reducing the number of times you smoke. You should be thinking about trying to quit the habit entirely.

Apart from Sodium, Potassium, and Phosphorus, You Should Reduce Protein Intake

When protein is consumed by the body, it breaks down into components called blood urea nitrogen, or BUN for short. The name of the components might sound a bit tacky, but their effect on your kidneys are rather serious. BUN is a difficult component for your kidneys to remove. The organs are not able to filter them properly. The less protein you eat, the less BUN is made in your body.

This does not mean that you have to reduce consuming proteins completely. It just means that you have to manage your protein intake.

## Special Tips for a Kidney-Friendly Lifestyle

A renal diet is not a one-time magic, which makes all your renal problems go away, as it is not a one-time formula; rather, it demands constant and consistent efforts to keep your kidneys healthy. This is imperative for renal disease patients, but it is equally important for those who don't want to bear the risks of future renal damage or failure. It is therefore advised to make this diet and renal friendly lifestyle a part of your routine. It can be easily adopted by following certain important steps like the following:

- While avoiding the intake of green leafy vegetables, you should increase the intake of other kidney-friendly veggies up to about 5-9 vegetables per day.
- Replace salt with other low sodium seasonings. There are certain market products that also contain a high amount of sodium like soy sauce or readymade broths or bouillon cubes; avoid their use as well.
- Meet your protein needs by consuming more white meat and plant-based sources. It is recommended to reduce the overall protein intake to a greater extent.
- Reduce all such triggers which can cause heart diseases like saturated fats and high sugar in your diet.
- You must also avoid food that can possibly contain pesticides and environmental contaminants.
- Instead of dining out and jeopardizing your health by eating unhealthy food, it is best to eat fresh and healthy food at home.
- Avoid the use of all such additives, which may contain a high amount of sodium, potassium, and phosphorous.
- Add plenty of low sodium drinks, especially water, to your diet.
- Obesity is another major cause of kidney disease; it is important to control your weight and attain a healthy body mass index-BMI.
- Excessive use of painkillers can also damage the kidneys, so avoid using such medicines.

# Chapter 6: Shopping list

It is best to consult with your doctor or dietician to come up with a proper shopping list when trying to live with chronic kidney disease. Below is a compiled list of items that can be bought at the grocery store and are considered kidney-friendly options. Most of the items on the list can be bought at any local grocery store but remember that fresh is always the best option. Try visiting your local farmers market for fresher alternatives. Make sure that you are asking about growing situations when purchasing that way because some fertilizers can introduce extra phosphates into the food. You want to keep the fruits or vegetables that you are buying as close to the principle of "farm to table" as you can. Fresher is better, but if you are stuck with cans, make sure there is nothing added to them, and they are as close to raw form as possible.

Even though these are just suggestions, it is always important for you to look at your labels and become acquainted with what the words mean and the servings you are looking at. Something may be low in sodium, but the serving size may be so small it doesn't make it worth it. Sometimes practicing self-control when using any kind of lifestyle change can be hard at first, so when starting out, it is important to carefully lay out all of the things that you are buying and cooking so that you can hold yourself accountable. Use the compilation below to make food conscious and kidney conscious choices.

### Juices
- Apricot
- Cranberry
- Cran-Apple
- Cran-Raspberry
- Grape
- Grapefruit
- Lemon
- Lemonade
- Papaya
- Pear
- Pineapple

### Other
- Coffee
- Club Soda
- Clear and Caffeine Soda Drinks
- Cream Soda
- Ginger Ale
- Fresh Brewed Teas

### Condiments/Sauces
- Chili Sauce
- BBQ
- Cornstarch
- Corn Syrup
- Mayonnaise or Salad Dressing
- Mustard
- Cream Cheese
- Honey
- Dry Tapioca
- Jam
- Jelly
- Ketchup
- Margarine
- Sugar Substitute
- Marmalade
- Taco Sauce
- Vinegar
- Worcestershire Sauce
- Steak Sauce

### Sweet Treats
- Lemon Flavored Cakes and Cookies
- Angel Food Cake
- Chewing Gum
- Vanilla Wafers
- Hard Candies

### Meat (Fresh)
- Beef
- Lamb
- Chicken
- Turkey
- Veal
- Pork
- Wild Caught Game (Like deer)

### Seafood
Fish (Fresh or Frozen)
Salmon
Shellfish
Lobster
Crab
Tuna (canned in water)

### Egg Substitutes
Tofu

### Dairy
Milk (limited to .5 cup a day)

### NonDairy Creamers
NonDairy Whipped Dessert Topping

### Milk Alternatives
Unenriched Almond
Unenriched Rice
Unenriched Soy

### Grains/Breads/Cereals (No Whole Wheat Options)
Bagels
Dinner Rolls
Flour Tortillas
English Muffins
Hamburger/Hot Dog Buns
Rice Cakes
Pita Bread
Sourdough
Rye
Melba Toasts

### Cereals that do not include dried fruits, nuts, or granola
Cream of Wheat
Cream of Rice
Grits

### Crackers
Animal Crackers
Graham Crackers (Honey or Cinnamon)
Oyster
Rusk
Low-Sodium Brown
Low-Sodium or Unsalted Saltines
Unsalted Pretzels
Wheat Thins (Low-Sodium)

### Pasta and Alternatives
Couscous
Lightly salted popcorn or unsalted popcorn
Macaroni
Spaghetti
White Rice
Egg Noodles

### Fruit
Cherries
Apples
Applesauce
Clementine Oranges
Apricots
Lemons
Blackberries
Boysenberries
Cranberries
Grapes
Grapefruit
Limes

Passion Fruit
Peaches
Pears

Mandarin Oranges
Pineapples
Strawberries

Raspberries
Plums
Tangerines

## Vegetables

Bean Sprouts
Alfalfa Sprouts
Bell Peppers (All Colors)
Asparagus
Cauliflower
Bamboo Shoots
Arugula
Broccoli
Cabbage
Carrots

Celery
Chives
Collard Greens
Egg Plant
Cucumber
Lettuce
Leeks
Kale
Mushrooms
Okra

Onion
Peas
Spinach
Spaghetti Squash
Zucchini
Yellow Squash
Radishes
Turnips

## Seasonings and Herbs

Allspice
Cloves
Cinnamon
Basil
Bay Leaf
Chili Powder
Celery Seed
Dry Mustard
Cilantro
Curry

Cumin
Marjoram
Dill
Extracts (Almond, Vanilla, Orange, Maple, Lemon, Peppermint)
Fennel
Sesame Seeds
Garlic
Ginger

Paprika
Mrs. Dash (Salt-Free and Low Sodium seasoning alternative)
Nutmeg
Pepper
Oregano
Parsley
Rosemary
Sage
Thyme

## Things to Avoid on a Renal Diet

Sodas that are dark in color
Avocado
Whole wheat breads and pastas
Brown rice
Bananas
Processed meats (lunchmeats, hotdogs, and bacon)
Pickles
Olives
Relish
Prepackaged meals

It cannot be reiterated enough that you need to be reading all the labels of the foods you are buying. Doing your own research before grocery shopping is your first line of defense in living a true kidney-friendly life. Make sure you are keeping an inventory of what you have and what you don't have because being proactive in your diet can help keep you from making an eating mistake in a pinch. Most of these items should have a place in your pantry or refrigerator. It is important that you keep up on your renal diet, and there is nothing to lose by including your family in the diet. It is never too early to start living a lifestyle that can improve your quality of life.

# 28 Day Meal Plan

| DAYS | BREAKFAST | LUNCH | DINNER | DESSERTS/SNACKS |
|---|---|---|---|---|
| 1 | Strawberry Muesli | Duck with Bok Choy | Artichoke Matzo Mina | ARTICHOKE MATZO MINA |
| 2 | Yogurt Bulgur | Grilled Duck Breast & Peach | Stuffed Zucchini Boats with Goat Cheese | STUFFED ZUCCHINI BOATS WITH GOAT CHEESE |
| 3 | Chia Pudding | Slow Cooker Turkey Legs | Greek Style Quesadillas | GREEK STYLE QUESADILLAS |
| 4 | Goat Cheese Omelet | Turkey and Cauliflower Soup | Creamy Penne | CREAMY PENNE |
| 5 | Rhubarb Muffins | Chicken Leftovers Chowder | Light Paprika Moussaka | LIGHT PAPRIKA MOUSSAKA |
| 6 | Winter Fruit Salad | Lamb & Pineapple Kebabs | Mackerel Skillet with Greens | MACKEREL SKILLET WITH GREENS |
| 7 | Buckwheat Granola | Baked Meatballs & Scallions | Basil Zucchini Spaghetti | BASIL ZUCCHINI SPAGHETTI |
| 8 | Mushroom Frittata | Stuffed Artichokes | Dill Carrots | DILL CARROTS |
| 9 | Breakfast Casserole | Ginger Cauliflower Rice | Herbed Vegetable Trout | HERBED VEGETABLE TROUT |
| 10 | Egg Pockets | Basil Zucchini Spaghetti | Citrus Glazed Salmon | CITRUS GLAZED SALMON |
| 11 | Italian Eggs with Peppers | Braised Cabbage | Broiled Salmon Fillets | BROILED SALMON FILLETS |
| 12 | Breakfast Crepes | Cauliflower and Leeks | Squash and Cranberries | SQUASH AND CRANBERRIES |
| 13 | Grilled Vegetables | Eggplant and Mushroom Sauté | Spicy Sweet Potatoes | SPICY SWEET POTATOES |
| 14 | Winter Berry Smoothie | Chicken Chili | Salmon Balls with Cream Cheese | SALMON BALLS WITH CREAM CHEESE |
| 15 | Kidney friendly Porridge | Lamb Stew | Fish Chili with Lentils | FISH CHILI WITH LENTILS |
| 16 | Zucchini and Egg Bowl | Sausage & Egg Soup | Chili Mussels | CHILI MUSSELS |
| 17 | Veggie Mix of Mediterranean | Mint Zucchini | Fried Scallops in Heavy Cream | FRIED SCALLOPS IN HEAVY CREAM |
| 18 | Veggies Mix of Colors | Celery and Kale Mix | Lettuce Seafood Wraps | LETTUCE SEAFOOD WRAPS |
| 19 | Chili Veggie and Quinoa Bowl | Kale, Mushrooms and Red Chard Mix | Mango Tilapia Fillets | MANGO TILAPIA FILLETS |
| 20 | Veggie Bowls | Carrot Casserole | Seafood Gratin | SEAFOOD GRATIN |

| 21 | Swiss Chard Bowls | Cauliflower Rice | Cabbage Beef Borscht | CABBAGE BEEF BORSCHT |
| --- | --- | --- | --- | --- |
| 22 | Rosemary Oats | Bok Choy And Beets | Lemon Pepper Beef Soup | LEMON PEPPER BEEF SOUP |
| 23 | Millet Muffins | Bok Choy and Beets | Cream of Crab Soup | CREAM OF CRAB SOUP |
| 24 | Kale Smoothie | Pork with Belle Pepper | Jamaican Drumsticks | JAMAICAN DRUMSTICKS |
| 25 | Apple Muesli | Pork with Pineapple | Chicken with Asparagus | CHICKEN WITH ASPARAGUS |
| 26 | Strawberry Muesli | Spiced Pork | Artichoke Matzo Mina | Green Coconut Smoothie |
| 27 | Yogurt Bulgur | Duck with Bok Choy | Stuffed Zucchini Boats with Goat Cheese | Coffee Brownies |
| 28 | Chia Pudding | Grilled Duck Breast & Peach | Greek Style Quesadillas | Avocado Mousse |

# Breakfast Recipes

## Strawberry Muesli

**Prep Time** 10 min  **Cook Time** 30 min  **Servings** 4

- 2 cups Greek yogurt
- 1 ½ cup strawberries, sliced
- 1 ½ cup Muesli
- 4 teaspoon maple syrup
- ¾ teaspoon ground cinnamon

Put Greek yogurt in the food processor.
Add 1 cup of strawberries, maple syrup, and ground cinnamon.
Blend the ingredients until you get smooth mass.
Transfer the yogurt mass in the serving bowls.
Add Muesli and stir well.
Leave the meal for 30 minutes in the fridge.
After this, decorate it with remaining sliced strawberries.

**Nutrition:** calories 149, fat 2.6, fiber 3.6, carbs 21.6, protein 12

## Yogurt Bulgur

**Prep Time** 10 min  **Cook Time** 15 min  **Servings** 3

- 1 cup bulgur
- 2 cups Greek yogurt
- 1 ½ cup water
- ½ teaspoon salt
- 1 teaspoon olive oil

Pour olive oil in the saucepan and add bulgur. Roast it over the medium heat for 2-3 minutes. Stir it from time to time.
After this, add salt and water.
Close the lid and cook bulgur for 15 minutes over the medium heat.
Then chill the cooked bulgur well and combine it with Greek yogurt. Stir it carefully.
Transfer the cooked meal into the serving plates. The yogurt bulgur tastes the best when it is cold.

**Nutrition:** calories 274, fat 4.9, fiber 8.5, carbs 40.8, protein 19.2

| Breakfast

## Chia Pudding

**Prep Time:** 10 min  
**Cook Time:** 30 min  
**Servings:** 2

- ½ cup raspberries
- 2 teaspoons maple syrup
- 1 ½ cup Plain yogurt
- ¼ teaspoon ground cardamom
- 1/3 cup Chia seeds, dried

Mix up together Plain yogurt with maple syrup and ground cardamom.
Add Chia seeds. Stir it gently.
Put the yogurt in the serving glasses and top with the raspberries.
Refrigerate the breakfast for at least 30 minutes or overnight.

**Nutrition:** calories 303, fat 11.2, fiber 11.8, carbs 33.2, protein 15.5

## Goat Cheese Omelet

**Prep Time:** 10 min  
**Cook Time:** 25 min  
**Servings:** 8

- 8 eggs, beaten
- 6 oz Goat cheese, crumbled
- ½ teaspoon salt
- 3 tablespoons sour cream
- 1 teaspoon butter
- ½ teaspoon canola oil
- ¼ teaspoon sage
- ¼ teaspoon dried oregano
- 1 teaspoon chives, chopped

Put butter in the skillet. Add canola oil and preheat the mixture until it is homogenous.
Meanwhile, in the mixing bowl combine together salt, sour cream, sage, dried oregano, and chives. Add eggs and stir the mixture carefully with the help of the spoon/fork.
Pour the egg mixture in the skillet with butter-oil liquid.
Sprinkle the omelet with goat cheese and close the lid.
Cook the breakfast for 20 minutes over the low heat. The cooked omelet should be solid. Slice it into the and transfer in the plates.

**Nutrition:** calories 176, fat 13.7, fiber 0, carbs 0, protein 12.2

**Renal Diet Cookbook for Beginners**

## Rhubarb Muffins

**Prep Time:** 10 min  
**Cook Time:** 25 min  
**Servings:** 8

- ½ cup almond meal
- 2 tablespoons crystallized ginger
- ¼ cup coconut sugar
- 1 tablespoon linseed meal
- ½ cup buckwheat flour
- ¼ cup brown rice flour
- 2 tablespoons powdered arrowroot
- 2 teaspoon gluten-free baking powder
- ½ teaspoon fresh grated ginger
- ½ teaspoon ground cinnamon
- 1 cup rhubarb, sliced
- 1 apple, cored, peeled and chopped
- 1/3 cup almond milk, unsweetened
- ¼ cup olive oil
- 1 free-range egg
- 1 teaspoon vanilla extract

In a bowl, mix the almond meal with the crystallized ginger, sugar, linseed meal, buckwheat flour, rice flour, arrowroot powder, grated ginger, baking powder and cinnamon and stir. In another bowl, mix the rhubarb with the apple, almond milk, oil, egg and vanilla and stir well. Combine the 2 mixtures, stir well, and divide into a lined muffin tray. Place in the oven at 350 degrees F and bake for 25 minutes. Serve the muffins for breakfast.
Enjoy!

**Nutrition:** calories 200, fat 4, fiber 6, carbs 13, protein 8

## Winter Fruit Salad

**Prep Time:** 10 min  
**Cook Time:** 0 min  
**Servings:** 6

- 4 persimmons, cubed
- 4 pears, cubed
- 1 cup grapes, halved
- 1 cup apples, peeled, cored and cubed
- ¾ cup pecans, halved
- 1 tablespoon olive oil
- 1 tablespoon peanut oil
- 1 tablespoon pomegranate flavored vinegar
- 2 tablespoons agave nectar

In a salad bowl, mix the persimmons with the pears, grapes, apples and pecans. In another bowl, mix the olive oil with the peanut oil, vinegar and agave nectar. Whisk well then pour over the salad, toss and serve for breakfast.
Enjoy!

**Nutrition:** calories 125, fat 3, fiber 6, carbs 14, protein 8

| Breakfast

## Buckwheat Granola

**Prep Time:** 10 min
**Cook Time:** 45 min
**Servings:** 6

- 2 cups oats
- 1 cup buckwheat
- 1 cup sunflower seeds
- 1 cup pumpkin seeds
- 1½ cups dates, pitted and chopped
- 1 cup apple puree
- 6 tablespoons coconut oil
- 5 tablespoons cocoa powder
- 1 teaspoon fresh grated ginger

In a large bowl, mix the oats with the buckwheat, sunflower seeds, pumpkin seeds, dates, apple puree, oil, cocoa powder and ginger then stir really well. Spread on a lined baking sheet, press well and place in the oven at 360 degrees F for 45 minutes. Leave the granola to cool down, slice and serve for breakfast.
Enjoy!

**Nutrition:** calories 161, fat 3, fiber 5, carbs 11, protein 7

## Mushroom Frittata

**Prep Time:** 10 min
**Cook Time:** 30 min
**Servings:** 4

- ¼ cup coconut milk, unsweetened
- 6 eggs
- 1 yellow onion, chopped
- 4 ounces white mushrooms, sliced
- 2 tablespoons olive oil
- 2 cups baby spinach
- A pinch of salt and black pepper

Heat up a pan with the oil over medium-high heat, add the onion, stir and cook for 2-3 minutes. Add the mushrooms, salt and pepper, stir and cook for 2 minutes more. In a bowl, mix the eggs with salt and pepper, stir well and pour over the mushrooms. Add the spinach, mix a bit, place in the oven and bake at 360 degrees F for 25 minutes. Slice the frittata and serve it for breakfast.
Enjoy!

**Nutrition:** calories 200, fat 3, fiber 6, carbs 14, protein 6

**Renal Diet Cookbook for Beginners**

## Breakfast Casserole

**Prep Time:** 15 min
**Cook Time:** 55 min
**Servings:** 9

- 8 oz. low fat sausage, crumbled
- 8 oz. cream cheese
- 1 cup almond milk
- 4 slices white bread, cut into cubes
- 5 eggs
- 1/2 teaspoon dry mustard
- 1/2 teaspoon dried onion flakes

Preheat your oven to 325 degrees F.
In a skillet, cook sausage in medium heat and then set aside.
In a blender, put the rest of the ingredients except the bread.
Pulse until well blended.
Pour mixture into a bowl.
Add the sausage.
Add mixture to a casserole dish.
Bake for 55 minutes.

**Nutrition:** Calories 224 /Protein 11 g /Carbohydrates 9 g /Fat 16 g / Cholesterol 149 mg /Sodium 356 mg / Potassium 201 mg /Phosphorus 159 mg /Calcium 97 mg /Fiber 0.4 g

## Egg Pockets

**Prep Time:** 15 min
**Cook Time:** 20 min
**Servings:** 4

- 1 teaspoon dry yeast
- 1 cup warm water
- 1 tablespoon oil
- 1 teaspoon garlic powder
- 2 cups all-purpose flour
- 1 tablespoon sugar
- 3 eggs, beat
- Cooking spray

Dissolve the yeast in water.
Add the oil, garlic powder, flour and sugar.
Form soft dough from the mixture.
Let it sit for 5 minutes.
Roll out the dough and slice into 4 portions.
Create a bowl with the dough.
Beat the eggs.
Put egg on top of the dough.
Fold the dough and pinch the edges.
Bake in the oven at 350 degrees F for 20 minutes.

**Nutrition:** Calories 321 /Protein 11 g /Carbohydrates 25 g /Fat 7 g / Cholesterol 123 mg /Sodium 50 mg /Potassium 139 mg /Phosphorus 130 mg /Calcium 30 mg /Fiber 2 g

| Breakfast

## Italian Eggs with Peppers

**Prep Time:** 15 min
**Cook Time:** 20 min
**Servings:** 6

- /2 cup onion, minced
- 1 cup red bell pepper, chopped
- 8 eggs, beaten
- Black pepper to taste
- 1/4 cup fresh basil, chopped

In a skillet, cook onion and red bell pepper until soft.
Season eggs with black pepper.
Pour egg mixture into the pan.
Cook without mixing until firm.
Sprinkle fresh basil on top before serving.

**Nutrition:** Calories 194 /Protein 13 g /Carbohydrates 5 g /Fat 14 g /Cholesterol 423 mg /Sodium 141 mg /Potassium 222 mg /Phosphorus 203 mg /Calcium 64 mg /Fiber 0.8 g

---

## Breakfast Crepes

**Prep Time:** 10 min
**Cook Time:** 10 min
**Servings:** 4

- 2 eggs
- 1 teaspoon vanilla extract
- ½ cup almond milk, unsweetened
- ½ cup water
- 2 tablespoons agave nectar
- 1 cup coconut flour
- 3 tablespoons coconut oil, melted

In a bowl, whisk the eggs with the vanilla extract, almond milk, water and agave nectar. Add the flour and 2 tablespoons oil gradually and stir until you obtain a smooth batter. Heat up a pan with the rest of the oil over medium heat, add some of the batter, spread into the pan and cook the crepe until it's golden on both sides then transfer to a plate. Repeat with the rest of the batter and serve the crepes for breakfast. Enjoy!

Nutrition: calories 121, fat 3, fiber 6, carbs 14, protein 6

Renal Diet Cookbook for Beginners

## Zucchini Fritters With Garlic Sauce

**Prep Time:** 6-7 min
**Cook Time:** 18 min
**Servings:** 4

- 1/4 red bell pepper (diced)
- 1/4 yellow bell pepper (diced)
- 1/4 green bell pepper (diced)
- 1/4 zucchini (diced)
- 1/4 red onion (diced)
- 1 teaspoon thyme, fresh or dried
- 1 teaspoon oregano
- 1 teaspoon extra virgin olive oil

Heat up the broiler to medium-high temperature. Soak diced vegetables in warm water before use. Mix up vegetables with oil and herbs in an oven dish and toss mixture. Cook under the broiler for about 12 minutes till vegetables are a bit grilled. The dish is ready can be severed singly or alternatively with salad or bread.

**Nutrition:** Calories 48, Fat 5, Fiber 10, Carbs 7, Protein 9

## Winter Berry Smoothie

**Prep Time:** 7-8 min
**Cook Time:** 130 min
**Servings:** 4

- 2 cups of water
- 1/4 cup cranberries
- 1/4 cup cherries (pitted)
- 1/4 cup blackberries

Add all cups of berries into a blender/smoothie maker. Blend to a smooth texture. Voila! Enjoy your rich breakfast.

Nutrition: Calories 21, Fat 2, Fiber 8, Carbs 6, Protein 5

| Breakfast

## Kidney Friendly Porridge

**Prep Time**: 7-8 min  
**Cook Time**: 12 min  
**Servings**: 2

- ½ cup cream wheat farina
- ½ cup canned pears (Sliced and drained)
- 1 cup water

Add a pinch of ground nutmeg to boiling water in a saucepan. Stop heating and gently add the cream wheat, while stirring till you have a good mix. Heat up the mixture and allow to boil. Reduce the heat and allow to cook for 4 minutes till it forms a thick texture. Add up canned pears and stir through.

**Nutrition**: Calories 215, Fat 3, Fiber 8, Carbs 45, Protein 6

---

## Zucchini and Egg Bowl

**Prep Time**: 8-9 min  
**Cook Time**: 125 min  
**Servings**: 4

- Salt and black pepper (a pinch)
- 4 tablespoons olive oil
- 2 tablespoons water
- 1 small avocado (pitted, peeled and chopped)
- 2 zucchinis (cut with a spiralizer)
- 2 eggs (whisked)
- 2 tablespoons green onions (chopped)
- 2 garlic cloves (minced)
- 2 sweet potatoes (Peeled and cubed)

Heat up a pan with olive oil added using medium heat. Pour in the chopped green onions, a pinch of salt and black pepper then stir and allow to cook for 5 minutes. Reduce heat. Add whisked eggs, water, cubed potatoes, cut zucchinis then toss and cook covered on high heat for 120 minutes. To serve, share mix into bowls and add avocado pieces to each, breakfast is served!

**Nutrition**: Calories 212, Fat 4, Fiber 8, Carbs 18, Protein 7

**Renal Diet Cookbook for Beginners**

## Veggie Mix of Mediterranean

**Prep Time** 10-11 min | **Cook Time** 35 min | **Servings** 4

- 4 cups baby arugula (torn)
- 1 tablespoon lemon juice
- 1 tablespoon olive oil
- 1 tablespoons oregano (chopped)
- Salt and black pepper (a pinch)
- Chili powder (a pinch)
- ½ teaspoon smoked paprika
- 2 cups quinoa (cooked)
- 1 eggplant (cubed)
- 2 zucchinis (cubed)
- For the sauce:
- ¾ cup of water
- ½ cup sesame seeds paste
- ½ teaspoon ground cumin
- 2 tablespoons lemon juice
- ½ teaspoon ground paprika
- 1 teaspoon red wine vinegar
- ¾ teaspoon harissa paste
- 1 teaspoon real maple syrup
- 1 garlic clove (minced)

Prepare a lined baking sheet and spread out the zucchini and eggplant in a line. Season with smoked paprika, chili powder, pepper, salt and olive oil. Coat in the seasonings added by tossing the mixture then heat in the oven at 400 degrees F for 30 minutes. Allow veggies to cool, place in a salad bowl. Add lemon juice, baby arugula, oregano, quinoa and oil. Mix. Using another bowl, whisk a mix of sesame paste with cumin, smoked paprika, harissa paste, maple syrup, garlic, vinegar, lemon juice and water. Pour the prepared mix over the salad and give it a toss. Your dish is ready! Enjoy.

**Nutrition:** Calories 212, Fat 4, Fiber 9, Carbs 18, Protein 7

## Veggies Mix of Colors

**Prep Time** 10-11 min | **Cook Time** 2 min | **Servings** 4

- 1½ cups coconut cream
- 2 tablespoons olive oil
- 1 garlic clove (minced)
- ¼ cup parsley (chopped)
- 1 jalapeno (chopped)
- 1 cup beans sprouts (soaked for 12 hours and drained)
- 1½ cups cucumbers (sliced)
- Handful basil (chopped)
- Salt and black pepper (a pinch)
- ½ cup of coconut milk
- 2 teaspoons white vinegar
- 1 teaspoon dill (chopped)
- 1 handful chives (chopped)
- 1 cup quinoa (cooked)
- 2 cups cherry tomatoes (halved)
- 1 tablespoon almonds (crushed)
- 2 avocados (peeled, pitted and cubed)

In a salad bowl, mix the quinoa with tomatoes, cucumbers, bean sprouts, basil, avocados, salt and pepper. In another bowl, whisk the oil with jalapeno, chives, parsley, dill, garlic, vinegar, coconut milk and cream. Add your mix into the salad mix and toss. Your breakfast is served!

**Nutrition:** Calories 185, Fat 4, Fiber 8, Carbs 18, Protein 7

| Breakfast

## Chili Veggie and Quinoa Bowl

**Prep Time:** 10-11 min
**Cook Time:** 2 min
**Servings:** 2

- 1 teaspoon sesame oil
- 1 teaspoon chili paste
- ½ cup quinoa (cooked)
- 1 sweet potato (peeled, cooked and cubed)
- 1 bunch broccolini (steamed)
- 2 tablespoons orange juice
- 2 carrots (shredded)
- ¼ cup pomegranate seeds
- A handful bean sprouts (soaked for 12 hours, drained)
- 1 teaspoon sesame seeds
- 1 tablespoon olive oil
- 1 teaspoon white vinegar
- 1 scallion (chopped)

Take a salad bowl and add the scallion with the sweet potato, broccolini, carrots, bean sprouts, pomegranate seeds, quinoa, oil and sesame seeds. In another bowl, whisk the sesame oil with chili paste, orange juice and vinegar. Add the chili mix with salad and toss together. Breakfast is served!

**Nutrition:** Calories 175, Fat 4, Fiber 7, Carbs 11, Protein 7

---

## Veggie Bowls

**Prep Time:** 10-11 min
**Cook Time:** 65 min
**Servings:** 2

- 1 avocado (peeled, pitted and cubed)
- 4 cups of water
- 1½ cups black barley
- 1 fennel bulb (shaved)
- 1 bunch watercress
- 1 orange, peeled and cut into segments
- 1 small red onion (sliced)
- ¼ cup walnuts
- 2 cups blueberries
- For the dressing:
- ½ cup of orange juice
- 1 small red onion, chopped
- 1 tablespoon raw honey
- Salt and black pepper (A pinch)
- ¼ cup olive oil
- 2 tablespoons red vinegar
- 1 teaspoon bee pollen

Into a small pot, add the barley. Add water and allow to simmer by cooking for 60 minutes. Drain and allow to cook in a salad bowl. Add the walnuts, avocado, red onion, watercress, orange, fennel and blueberries and toss. In another bowl, create a mix of orange juice with honey, oil, pepper, salt, bee pollen, vinegar, and onion. Dish out the salad. Enjoy your dish!

**Nutrition:** Calories 212, Fat 14, Fiber 6, Carbs 15, Protein 7

Renal Diet Cookbook for Beginners

## Swiss Chard Bowls

**Prep Time** 10-11 min  **Cook Time** 6 min  **Servings** 4

- 1 garlic clove (minced)
- 1 cup quinoa (cooked)
- 1 carrot (shredded)
- 1 roasted red pepper (cubed)
- 2 teaspoons lemon juice
- 4 eggs (fried)
- 1 bunch Swiss chard (chopped)
- 2 teaspoons of olive oil
- ½ cup cherry tomatoes (halved)
- 1 green onion (chopped)
- Salt and black pepper (A pinch)

Heat up a pan with olive oil added using medium heat. Add up the chard and allow to cook for 3 minutes. Pour in the onions, garlic, red pepper, tomatoes, carrot with a pinch of salt and pepper. Toss a bot and allow to cook for 3-4 minutes more. Pour in the lemon juice and quinoa then cook for 60 seconds. Divide into bowls and top each with a fried egg. Enjoy your dish!

**Nutrition:** Calories 203, Fat 4, Fiber 6, Carbs 14, Protein 7

## Rosemary Oats

**Prep Time** 9-10 min  **Cook Time** 18 min  **Servings** 2

- Salt and black pepper (A pinch)
- ½ cup oats
- ½ cup of water
- ½ teaspoon coconut oil (melted)
- ½ cup almond milk (unsweetened)
- ½ cup chopped onion
- ½ cup chopped collard greens
- ½ cup chopped tomato
- ½ cup sliced white mushrooms
- ½ tablespoon chopped rosemary

Heat up a pan with coconut oil added using medium heat. Add the chopped onions, stir and cook for 60 seconds. Pour in the collard greens, tomato, rosemary, mushrooms with a pinch of salt and pepper, stir and cook for 5 minutes before turning off the heat. Take another pot mediumly heated and heat up continuously with almond milk and water. Pour the collard green mix into the pan with the oats, stir and cook for 5 minutes more. Serve as desired.

**Nutrition:** Calories 203, Fat 4, Fiber 6, Carbs 14, Protein 7

| Breakfast

## Millet Muffins

**Prep Time:** 10 min
**Cook Time:** 15 min
**Servings:** 12

- ¼ cup coconut oil, melted
- 1 egg
- ½ teaspoon vanilla extract
- 1 teaspoon baking powder
- 1½ cups organic millet, cooked
- ½ cup coconut sugar
- Cooking spray

In a blender, blend the melted coconut oil with the egg, vanilla extract, baking powder, millet and sugar. Grease a muffin tray with cooking spray and divide the millet mix into each cup. Place the muffins in the oven and bake at 350 degrees F for 30 minutes. Let the muffins cool and then serve!
Enjoy!

**Nutrition:** calories 167, fat 4, fiber 7, carbs 15, protein 6

## Kale Smoothie

**Prep Time:** 10 min
**Cook Time:** 0 min
**Servings:** 5

- 10 kale leaves
- 5 bananas, peeled and cut into chunks
- 2 pears, chopped
- 5 tablespoons almond butter
- 5 cups almond milk

In your blender, mix the kale with the bananas, pears, almond butter and almond milk, pulse well, divide into glasses and serve for breakfast.
Enjoy!

**Nutrition:** calories 267, fat 11, fiber 7, carbs 15, protein 7

**Renal Diet Cookbook for Beginners**

## Apple Muesli

**Prep Time:** 10 min
**Cook Time:** 0 min
**Servings:** 4

- 2 apples, peeled, cored and grated
- 1 cup rolled oats
- 3 tablespoons flax seeds
- 1¼ cups coconut cream
- 1¼ cups coconut water
- ½ cup goji berries
- 2 tablespoons chopped mint
- 3 tablespoons raw honey

In a bowl, mix the apples with the oats, flax seeds, coconut cream, coconut water, goji berries, mint and honey. Stir well, divide into smaller bowls and serve for breakfast. Enjoy!

**Nutrition:** calories 171, fat 2, fiber 6, carbs 14, protein 5

# Lunch

## Duck with Bok Choy

**Prep Time** 15 min  **Cook Time** 12 min  **Servings** 4-6

- 2 tablespoons coconut oil
- 1 onion, sliced thinly
- 2 teaspoons fresh ginger, grated finely
- 2 minced garlic cloves
- 1 tablespoon fresh orange zest, grated finely
- ¼ cup chicken broth
- 2/3 cup fresh orange juice
- 1 roasted duck, meat picked
- 3-pound Bok choy leaves
- 1 orange, peeled, seeded and segmented

In a sizable skillet, melt coconut oil on medium heat.
Add onion, ginger and garlic and sauté for around 3 minutes.
Add ginger and garlic and sauté for about 1-2 minutes.
Stir in orange zest, broth and orange juice.
Add duck meat and cook for around 3 minutes.
Transfer the meat pieces in a plate.
Add Bok choy and cook for about 3-4 minutes.
Divide Bok choy mixture in serving plates and top with duck meat.
Serve with the garnishing of orange segments.

**Per serving:** Calories: 433, Fat: 12g, Carbohydrates: 21g, Fiber: 9g, Protein: 34g

## Grilled Duck Breast & Peach

**Prep Time** 15 min  **Cook Time** 24 min  **Servings** 4-6

- 2 shallots, sliced thinly
- 2 tablespoons fresh ginger, minced
- 2 tablespoons fresh thyme, chopped
- Salt and freshly ground black pepper, to taste
- 2 duck breasts
- 2 peaches, pitted and quartered
- ½ teaspoon ground fennel seeds
- ½ tablespoon extra-virgin olive oil

In a substantial bowl, mix together shallots, ginger, thyme, salt and black pepper.
Add duck breasts and coat with marinade evenly.
Refrigerate to marinate for about 2-12 hours.
Preheat the grill to medium-high heat. Grease the grill grate.
In a sizable bowl, add peaches, fennel seeds, salt, black pepper and oil and toss to coat well.
Place the duck breast on grill, skin side down and grill for around 6-8 minutes per side.
Transfer the duck breast onto a plate.
Now, grill the peaches for around 3 minutes per side.
Serve the duck breasts with grilled peaches.

**Per serving:** Calories: 450, Fat: 14g, Carbohydrates: 25g, Fiber: 12g, Protein: 42g

## Slow Cooker Turkey Legs

**Prep Time** 10 min  **Cook Time** 50 min  **Servings** 2

- 2 turkey legs
- 1 tablespoon mustard
- 1 tablespoon butter
- 1/2 teaspoon smoked paprika
- 1 teaspoon dried rosemary
- Salt and pepper, to taste
- 1 chopped leek
- 1/2 teaspoon minced garlic
- For the Gravy:
- 1/2 stick butter
- 1 cup heavy cream
- Salt and pepper, to taste

Rub turkey legs with the mustard and butter. Preheat a skillet over a medium-high heat Fry the turkey legs on all sides, making sure that they are brown all over.
Put the turkey legs in the slow cooker, but keep the fat to one side. Add the paprika, rosemary, pepper, salt, leeks and garlic.
Put the slow cooker on low and cook for 6 hours.
Heat the reserved fat with 1/2 stick of butter on a medium flame. Add the cream to the fat and stir until the mixture is hot.
Add salt and pepper and stir until the sauce is thickened and hot. Serve the sauce on top of the chicken drumsticks. Enjoy.

**Per serving:** Calories280 ,Protein 15.8g ,Fat 22.2g ,Carbs 4.3g ,Sugar 1.7g

---

## Turkey and Cauliflower Soup

**Prep Time** 10 min  **Cook Time** 50 min  **Servings** 2

- 2 tablespoons coconut oil
- 2 chopped garlic cloves
- 2 chopped shallots
- 4 ½ cups chicken stock
- 1/2 head cauliflower florets
- 1 pound turkey thighs
- 2 bay leaves
- 1 rosemary sprig
- 1/2 teaspoon celery seeds
- Salt and ground black pepper, to taste
- 1/2 teaspoon cayenne pepper
- 4 dollops of sour cream

Preheat a heavy pot over a medium flame and heat the oil. Sauté the garlic and shallots until they are fragrant.
Pour in the chicken stock and bring to the boil.
Add the turkey, cauliflower, bay leaves, celery seeds, rosemary, salt, pepper and cayenne pepper.
Simmer on a moderate-low heat for 25 – 30 minutes.
Pour the soup into 4 bowls and put a dollop of sour cream on each Enjoy!

**Per serving:** Calories274, Protein 26.7g ,Fat 14.4g ,Carbs 5.6g ,Sugar 3.1g

| Lunch

## Chicken Leftovers Chowder

**Prep Time** 10 min  
**Cook Time** 50 min  
**Servings** 2

- 2 tablespoons coconut oil
- 2 roughly chopped cloves of garlic
- A bunch of chopped scallions
- 1/2 pound shredded and skinned leftover roast chicken
- 2 rosemary sprigs
- 1 bay leaf
- 1 thyme sprig
- 1 tablespoon chicken bouillon granules
- 3 cups water
- 1/2 cup whipped cream
- 1 1/2 cups milk
- 1 lightly beaten whole egg
- 1 tablespoons dry sherry

Preheat a stockpot over a moderate flame and melt the coconut oil. Sauté the garlic and scallions until softened and fragrant.
Add the chicken, rosemary, bay leaf, thyme, chicken bouillon granules and water. Partially cover and bring to the boil. Then simmer for 20 minutes.
Turn the heat down to low and add the whipped cream and milk. Simmer until it has thickened. Put in the egg and stir for a couple of minutes.
Taste to make sure the seasoning is right. Ladle into individual bowls and drizzle each with the sherry. Enjoy!

**Per serving:** Calories350 ,Protein 20g ,Fat 25.8g ,Carbs 5.5g ,Sugar 2.8g

## Lamb & Pineapple Kebabs

**Prep Time** 15 min  
**Cook Time** 10 min  
**Servings** 4-6

- 1 large pineapple, cubed into 1½-inch size, divided
- 1 (½-inch) piece fresh ginger, chopped
- 2 garlic cloves, chopped
- Salt, to taste
- 16-24-ounce lamb shoulder steak, trimmed and cubed into 1½-inch size
- Fresh mint leaves coming from a bunch
- Ground cinnamon, to taste

In a blender, add about 1½ of pineapple, ginger, garlic and salt and pulse till smooth. Transfer the amalgamation right into a large bowl.
Add chops and coat with mixture generously. Refrigerate to marinate for about 1-2 hours.
Preheat the grill to medium heat. Grease the grill grate.
Thread lam, remaining pineapple and mint leaves onto pre-soaked wooden skewers.
Grill the kebabs approximately 10 min, turning occasionally.

**Per serving:** Calories: 482, Fat: 16g, Carbohydrates: 22g, Fiber: 5g, Protein: 377g

**Renal Diet Cookbook for Beginners |**

## Baked Meatballs & Scallions

**Prep Time:** 20 min  
**Cook Time:** 35 min  
**Servings:** 4-6

**For Meatballs:**
- 1 lemongrass stalk, outer skin peeled and chopped
- 1 (1½-inch) piece fresh ginger, sliced
- 3 garlic cloves, chopped
- 1 cup fresh cilantro leaves, chopped roughly
- ½ cup fresh basil leaves, chopped roughly
- 2 tablespoons plus 1 teaspoon fish sauce
- 2 tablespoons water
- 2 tablespoons fresh lime juice
- ½ pound lean ground pork
- 1-pound lean ground lamb
- 1 carrot, peeled and grated
- 1 organic egg, beaten

**For Scallions:**
- 16 stalks scallions, trimmed
- 2 tablespoons coconut oil, melted
- Salt, to taste
- ½ cup water

Preheat the oven to 375 degrees F. Grease a baking dish.

In a blender, add lemongrass, ginger, garlic, fresh herbs, fish sauce, water and lime juice and pulse till chopped finely.

Transfer the amalgamation in a bowl with remaining ingredients and mix till well combined.

Make about 1-inch balls from mixture.

Arrange the balls into prepared baking dish in a single layer.

In another rimmed baking dish, arrange scallion stalks in a very single layer.

Drizzle with coconut oil and sprinkle with salt.

Pour water in the baking dish 1nd with a foil paper cover it tightly.

Bake the scallion for around a half-hour.

Bake the meatballs for approximately 30-35 minutes.

**Per serving:** Calories: 432, Fat: 13g, Carbohydrates: 25g, Fiber: 8g, Protein: 40g

---

## Stuffed Artichokes

**Prep Time:** 10 min  
**Cook Time:** 1 h 10 min  
**Servings:** 4

- 4 artichokes, stems cut off and hearts chopped
- 3 garlic cloves, minced
- 2 cups spinach, chopped
- 1 tablespoon coconut oil, melted
- 1 yellow onion, chopped
- 4 ounces shallots, chopped, cooked and crumbled
- A pinch of black pepper

Put artichokes in a large saucepan, add water to cover, bring to a boil over medium heat, cook for 30 minutes, drain them and leave them aside to cool down.

Heat up a pan with the oil over medium high heat, add onion, stir and cook for 10 minutes. Add spinach, stir, cook for 3 minutes, take off heat and leave aside to cool down.

Put cooked shallots in your food processor, add artichoke insides as well and pulse well. Add this to spinach and onion mix and stir well.

Place artichoke cups on a lined baking sheet, stuff them with spinach mix, place in the oven at 375 degrees F and bake for 30 minutes.

Divide the artichokes between plates and serve as a side dish.

Enjoy!

**Per serving:** Calories 144, Fat 3,8, Fiber 9,7, Carbs 25,6, Protein 6,9

| Lunch

# Ginger Cauliflower Rice

**Prep Time:** 10 min
**Cook Time:** 10 min
**Servings:** 4

- 5 cups cauliflower florets
- 3 tablespoons coconut oil
- 4 ginger slices, grated
- 1 tablespoon coconut vinegar
- 3 garlic cloves, minced
- 1 tablespoon chives, minced
- A pinch of sea salt
- Black pepper to taste

Put cauliflower florets in a food processor and pulse well.
Heat up a pan with the oil over medium-high heat, add ginger, stir and cook for 3 minutes.
Add cauliflower rice and garlic, stir and cook for 7 minutes.
Add salt, black pepper, vinegar, and chives, stir, cook for a few seconds more, divide between plates and serve.
Enjoy!

**Per serving:** Calories 125, Fat 10,4, Fiber 3,2, Carbs 7,9, Protein 2,7

# Basil Zucchini Spaghetti

**Prep Time:** 1 h 10 min
**Cook Time:** 10 min
**Servings:** 4

- 1/3 cup coconut oil, melted
- 4 zucchinis, cut with a spiralizer
- ¼ cup basil, chopped
- A pinch of sea salt
- Black pepper to taste
- ½ cup walnuts, chopped
- 2 garlic cloves, minced

In a bowl, mix zucchini spaghetti with salt and pepper, toss to coat, leave aside for 1 hour, drain well and put in a bowl.
Heat up a pan with the oil over medium-high heat, add zucchini spaghetti and garlic, stir and cook for 5 minutes.
Add basil and walnuts and black pepper, stir and cook for 3 minutes more.
Divide between plates and serve as a side dish
Enjoy!

**Per serving:** Calories 287, Fat 27,8, Fiber 3,3, Carbs 8,7, Protein 6,3

## Braised Cabbage

**Prep Time** 10 min

**Cook Time** 10 min

**Servings** 4

- 1 small cabbage head, shredded
- 2 tablespoons water
- A drizzle of olive oil
- 6 ounces shallots, cooked and chopped
- A pinch of black pepper
- A pinch of sweet paprika
- 1 tablespoon dill, chopped

Heat up a pan with the oil over medium heat, add the cabbage and the water, stir and sauté for 5 minutes.
Add the rest of the ingredients, toss, cook for 5 minutes more, divide everything between plates and serve as a side dish!
Enjoy!

**Per serving:** Calories 91, Fat 0,5, Fiber 5,8, Carbs 20,8, Protein 4,1

## Cauliflower and Leeks

**Prep Time** 10 min

**Cook Time** 20 min

**Servings** 4

- 1 and ½ cups leeks, chopped
- 1 and ½ cups cauliflower florets
- 2 garlic cloves, minced
- 1 and ½ cups artichoke hearts
- 2 tablespoons coconut oil, melted
- Black pepper to taste

Heat up a pan with the oil over medium-high heat, add garlic, leeks, cauliflower florets and artichoke hearts, stir and cook for 20 minutes.
Add black pepper, stir, divide between plates and serve.
Enjoy!

**Per serving:** Calories 192, Fat 6,9, Fiber 8,2, Carbs 35,1, Protein 5,1

| Lunch

# Eggplant and Mushroom Sauté

**Prep Time:** 10 min
**Cook Time:** 30 min
**Servings:** 4

- 2 pounds oyster mushrooms, chopped
- 6 ounces shallots, peeled, chopped
- 1 yellow onion, chopped
- 2 eggplants, cubed
- 3 celery stalks, chopped
- 1 tablespoon parsley, chopped
- A pinch of sea salt
- Black pepper to taste
- 1 tablespoon savory, dried
- 3 tablespoons coconut oil, melted

Heat up a pan with the oil over medium high heat, add onion, stir and cook for 4 minutes.
Add shallots, stir and cook for 4 more minutes.
Add eggplant pieces, mushrooms, celery, savory and black pepper to taste, stir and cook for 15 minutes.
Add parsley, stir again, cook for a couple more minutes, divide between plates and serve.
Enjoy!

**Per serving:** Calories 1013, Fat 10,9, Fiber 35,5, Carbs 156,5, Protein 69,1

---

# Chicken Chili

**Prep Time:** 20 min
**Cook Time:** 1 h 15 min
**Servings:** 8

- 1 tablespoon oil
- 1 cup onion, chopped
- 4 garlic cloves, chopped
- 1 cup green pepper
- 1 cup celery, chopped
- 1 cup carrots, chopped
- 14 oz. low-sodium chicken broth
- 1 lb. chicken breast, cubed and cooked
- 1 cup low-sodium tomatoes, drained and iced
- 1 cup kidney beans, rinsed and drained
- 3/4 cup salsa
- 3 tablespoons chili powder
- 1 teaspoon ground oregano
- 4 cups white rice, cooked

In a pot, pour oil and cook onion, garlic, green pepper, celery and carrots.
Add the broth.
Bring to a boil.
Add the rest of the ingredients except the rice.
Simmer for 1 hour.
Serve with rice.

**Per serving:** Calories 355, Protein 24 g, Carbohydrates 38 g, Fat 12 g, Cholesterol 59 mg, Sodium 348 mg, Potassium 653 mg, Phosphorus 270 mg, Calcium 133 mg, Fiber 4.7 g

## Lamb Stew

**Prep Time:** 30 min
**Cook Time:** 1 h 40 min
**Servings:** 6

- 1 lb. boneless lamb shoulder, trimmed and cubes
- Black pepper to taste
- 1/4 cup all-purpose flour
- 1 tablespoon olive oil
- 1 onion, chopped
- 3 garlic cloves, chopped
- 1/2 cup tomato sauce
- 2 cups low-sodium beef broth
- 1 teaspoon dried thyme
- 2 parsnips, sliced
- 2 carrots, sliced
- 1 cup frozen peas

Season lamb with pepper.
Coat evenly with flour.
Pour oil in a pot over medium heat.
Cook the lamb and then set aside.
Add onion to the pot.
Cook for 2 minutes.
Add garlic and saute for 30 seconds.
Pour in the broth to deglaze the pot.
Add the tomato sauce and thyme.
Put the lamb back to the pot.
Bring to a boil and then simmer for 1 hour.
Add parsnips and carrots.
Cook for 30 minutes.
Add green peas and cook for 5 minutes.

**Per serving:** Calories 283, Protein 27 g, Carbohydrates 19 g, Fat 11 g, Cholesterol 80 mg, Sodium 325 mg, Potassium 527 mg, Phosphorus 300 mg, Calcium 56 mg, Fiber 3.4 g

---

## Sausage & Egg Soup

**Prep Time:** 15 min
**Cook Time:** 30 min
**Servings:** 4

- 1/2 lb. ground beef
- Black pepper
- 1/2 teaspoon ground sage
- 1/2 teaspoon garlic powder
- 1/2 teaspoon dried basil
- 4 slices bread (one day old), cubed
- 2 tablespoons olive oil
- 1 tablespoon herb seasoning blend
- 2 garlic cloves, minced
- 3 cups low-sodium chicken broth
- 1 cup water
- 4 tablespoons fresh parsley
- 4 eggs
- 2 tablespoons Parmesan cheese, grated

Preheat your oven to 375 degrees F.
Mix the first five ingredients to make the sausage.
Toss bread cubes in oil and seasoning blend.
Bake in the oven for 8 minutes. Set aside.
Cook the sausage in a pan over medium heat.
Cook the garlic in the sausage drippings for 2 minutes.
Stir in the broth, water and parsley.
Bring to a boil and then simmer for 10 minutes.
Pour into serving bowls and top with baked bread, egg and sausage.

**Per serving:** Calories 335, Protein 26 g, Carbohydrates 15 g, Fat 19 g, Cholesterol 250 mg, Sodium 374 mg, Potassium 392 mg, Phosphorus 268 mg, Calcium 118 mg, Fiber 0.9 g

| Lunch

## Mint Zucchini

**Prep Time:** 10 min
**Cook Time:** 7 min
**Servings:** 4

- 2 tablespoons mint
- 2 zucchinis, halved lengthwise and then slice into half moons
- 1 tablespoon coconut oil, melted
- ½ tablespoon dill, chopped
- A pinch of cayenne pepper

Heat up a pan with the oil over medium-high heat, add zucchinis, stir and cook for 6 minutes.
Add cayenne, dill and mint, stir, cook for 1 minute more, divide between plates and serve.
Enjoy!

**Per serving:** Calories 46, Fat 3,6, Fiber 1,3, Carbs 3,5, Protein 1,3

---

## Celery and Kale Mix

**Prep Time:** 10 min
**Cook Time:** 20 min
**Servings:** 4

- 2 celery stalks, chopped
- 5 cups kale, torn
- 1 small red bell pepper, chopped
- 3 tablespoons water
- 1 tablespoon coconut oil, melted

Heat up a pan with the oil over medium-high heat, add celery, stir and cook for 10 minutes. Add kale, water, and bell pepper, stir and cook for 10 minutes more.
Divide between plates and serve.
Enjoy!

**Per serving:** Calories 81, fat 3,5, Fiber 1,8, Carbs 11,3, Protein 2,9

**Renal Diet Cookbook for Beginners |**

## Kale, Mushrooms and Red Chard Mix

**Prep Time:** 10 min
**Cook Time:** 17 min
**Servings:** 4

- ½ pound brown mushrooms, sliced
- 5 cups kale, roughly chopped
- 1 and ½ tablespoons coconut oil
- 3 cups red chard, chopped
- 2 tablespoons water
- Black pepper to taste

Heat up a pan with the oil over medium high heat, add mushrooms, stir and cook for 5 minutes.
Add red chard, kale and water, stir and cook for 10 minutes.
Add black pepper to taste, stir and cook 2 minutes more.
Divide between plates and serve.
Enjoy!

**Per serving:** Calories 97, Fat 3,4, Fiber 2,3, Carbs 13,3, Protein 5,4

---

## Carrot Casserole

**Prep Time:** 10 min
**Cook Time:** 20 min
**Servings:** 8

- 1 lb. carrots, sliced into rounds
- 12 low-sodium crackers
- 2 tablespoons butter
- 2 tablespoons onion, chopped
- 1/4 cup cheddar cheese, shredded

Preheat your oven to 350 degrees F.
Boil carrots in a pot of water until tender.
Drain the carrots and reserve ¼ cup liquid.
Mash carrots.
Add all the ingredients into the carrots except cheese.
Place the mashed carrots in a casserole dish.
Sprinkle cheese on top and bake in the oven for 15 minutes.

**Per serving:** Calories 94, Protein 2 g, Carbohydrates 9 g, Fat 6 g, Cholesterol 13 mg, Sodium 174 mg, Potassium 153 mg, Phosphorus 47 mg, Calcium 66 mg, Fiber 1.8 g

| Lunch

## Cauliflower Rice

**Prep Time:** 10 min
**Cook Time:** 10 min
**Servings:** 4

- 1 head cauliflower, sliced into florets
- 1 tablespoon butter
- Black pepper to taste
- 1/4 teaspoon garlic powder
- 1/4 teaspoon herb seasoning blend

Put cauliflower florets in a food processor. Pulse until consistency is similar to grain.
In a pan over medium heat, melt the butter and add the spices.
Toss cauliflower rice and cook for 10 minutes.
Fluff using a fork before serving.

**Per serving:** Calories 47, Protein 1 g, Carbohydrates 4 g, Fat 3 g, Cholesterol 8 mg, Sodium 43 mg, Potassium 206 mg, Phosphorus 31 mg, Calcium 16 mg, Fiber 1.4 g

---

## Bok Choy And Beets

**Prep Time:** 10 min
**Cook Time:** 30 min
**Servings:** 4

- 1 tablespoon coconut oil
- 4 cups bok choy, chopped
- 3 beets, cut into quarters and thinly sliced
- 2 tablespoons water
- A pinch of cayenne pepper

Put water in a large saucepan, add the beets, bring to a boil over medium heat, cover, cook for 20 minutes and drain.
Heat up a pan with the oil over medium high heat, add the bok choy and the water, stir and cook for 10 minutes.
Add beets and cayenne pepper, stir, cook for 2 minutes more, divide between plates and serve as a side dish!
Enjoy!

**Per serving:** Calories 71, Fat 3,7, Fiber 2,2, Carbs 9, Protein 2,3

**Renal Diet Cookbook for Beginners | 51**

## Pork with Bell Pepper

**Prep Time** 15 min  **Cook Time** 13 min  **Servings** 4

- 1 tablespoon fresh ginger, chopped finely
- 4 garlic cloves, chopped finely
- 1 cup fresh cilantro, chopped and divided
- ¼ cup plus 1 tbsp olive oil, divided
- 1-pound tender pork, trimmed, sliced thinly
- 2 onions, sliced thinly
- 1 green bell pepper, seeded and sliced thinly
- 1 tablespoon fresh lime juice

In a substantial bowl, mix together ginger, garlic, ½ cup of cilantro and ¼ cup of oil.
Add pork and coat with mixture generously.
Refrigerate to marinate approximately a couple of hours.
Heat a big skillet on medium-high heat.
Add pork mixture and stir fry for approximately 4-5 minutes.
Transfer the pork right into a bowl.
In the same skillet, heat remaining oil on medium heat.
Add onion and sauté for approximately 3 minutes.
Stir in bell pepper and stir fry for about 3 minutes.
Stir in pork, lime juice and remaining cilantro and cook for about 2 minutes.
Serve hot.

**Per serving:** Calories: 429, Fat: 19g, Carbohydrates: 26g, Fiber: 9g, Protein: 35g

---

## Pork with Pineapple

**Prep Time** 15 min  **Cook Time** 14 min  **Servings** 4

- 2 tablespoons coconut oil
- 1½ pound pork tenderloin, trimmed and cut into bite-sized pieces
- 1 onion, chopped
- 2 minced garlic cloves
- 1 (1-inch) piece fresh ginger, minced
- 20-ounce pineapple, cut into chunks
- 1 large red bell pepper, seeded and chopped
- ¼ cup fresh pineapple juice
- ¼ cup coconut aminos
- Salt and freshly ground black pepper, to taste

In a substantial skillet, melt coconut oil on high heat.
Add pork and stir fry approximately 4-5 minutes.
Transfer the pork right into a bowl.
In exactly the same skillet, heat remaining oil on medium heat.
Add onion, garlic and ginger and sauté for around 2 minutes.
Stir in pineapple and bell pepper and stir fry for around 3 minutes.
Stir in pork, pineapple juice and coconut aminos and cook for around 3-4 minutes.
Serve hot.

**Per serving:** Calories: 431, Fat: 10g, Carbohydrates: 22g, Fiber: 8g, Protein: 33g

| Lunch

# Spiced Pork

**Prep Time:** 15 min
**Cook Time:** 1 h 52 min
**Servings:** 6

- 1 (2-inch) piece fresh ginger, chopped
- 5-10 garlic cloves, chopped
- 1 teaspoon ground cumin
- ½ teaspoon ground turmeric
- 1 tablespoon hot paprika
- 1 tablespoon red pepper flakes
- Salt, to taste
- 2 tablespoons cider vinegar
- 2-pounds pork shoulder, trimmed and cubed into 1½-inch size
- 2 cups domestic hot water, divided
- 1 (1-inch wide) ball tamarind pulp
- ¼ cup olive oil
- 1 teaspoon black mustard seeds, crushed
- 4 green cardamoms
- 5 whole cloves
- 1 (3-inch) cinnamon stick
- 1 cup onion, chopped finely
- 1 large red bell pepper, seeded and chopped

In a food processor, add ginger, garlic, cumin, turmeric, paprika, red pepper flakes, salt and cider vinegar and pulse till smooth.
Transfer the amalgamation in to a large bowl.
Add pork and coat with mixture generously.
Keep aside, covered for around an hour at room temperature.
In a bowl, add 1 cup of warm water and tamarind and make aside till water becomes cool.
With the hands, crush the tamarind to extract the pulp.
Add remaining cup of hot water and mix till well combined.
Through a fine sieve, strain the tamarind juice inside a bowl.
In a sizable skillet, heat oil on medium-high heat.
Add mustard seeds, green cardamoms, cloves and cinnamon stick and sauté for about 4 minutes.
Add onion and sauté for approximately 5 minutes.
Add pork and stir fry for approximately 6 minutes.
Stir in tamarind juice and convey with a boil.
Reduce the heat to medium-low and simmer 1½ hours.
Stir in bell pepper and cook for about 7 minutes.

**Per serving:** Calories: 435, Fat: 16g, Carbohydrates: 27g, Fiber: 3g, Protein: 39g

# Dinner

## Artichoke Matzo Mina

**Prep Time** 10 min

**Cook Time** 45 min

**Servings** 6

- 4 sheets matzo
- ½ cup artichoke hearts, canned
- 1 cup cream cheese
- 1 cup spinach, chopped
- ½ teaspoon salt
- 1 teaspoon ground black pepper
- 3 tablespoons fresh dill, chopped
- 3 eggs, beaten
- 1 teaspoon canola oil
- ½ cup cottage cheese

In the bowl combine together cream cheese, spinach, salt, ground black pepper, dill, and cottage cheese.
Pour canola oil in the skillet, add artichoke hearts and roast them for 2-3 minutes over the medium heat. Stir them from time to time. Then add roasted artichoke hearts in the cheese mixture.
Add eggs and stir until homogenous.
Place one sheet of matzo in the casserole mold.
Then spread it with cheese mixture generously. Cover the cheese layer with the second sheet of matzo.
Repeat the steps till you use all ingredients.
Then preheat oven to 360F.
Bake matzo mina for 40 minutes.
Cut the cooked meal into the.

**Per serving:** Calories 272, Fat 17.3, Fiber 4.3, Carbs 20.2, Protein 11.8

## Stuffed Zucchini Boats with Goat Cheese

**Prep Time** 15 min

**Cook Time** 30 min

**Servings** 4

- 1 cup ground chicken
- 3 oz goat cheese, crumbled
- 2 zucchinis, trimmed
- 1 tablespoon sour cream
- ½ teaspoon salt
- ½ teaspoon chili flakes
- ½ teaspoon dried oregano
- 1 tablespoon tomato sauce
- 4 teaspoons butter

Cut zucchini into lengthwise boards.
Scoop the zucchini meat.
Then mix up together ground chicken, goat cheese, salt, chili flakes, dried oregano, and fill the zucchini boats.
Then top them with sour cream and butter.
Wrap zucchini boats in the foil and transfer in the preheated to the 360F oven.
Bake zucchini for 30 minutes.
Then discard the foil and transfer cooked zucchini boats in the serving plates.

**Per serving:** Calories 220, Fat 14.8, Fiber 1.2, Carbs 4.2, Protein 18

## Greek Style Quesadillas

**Prep Time:** 10 min
**Cook Time:** 10 min
**Servings:** 4

- 4 whole wheat tortillas
- 1 cup Mozzarella cheese, shredded
- 1 cup fresh spinach, chopped
- 2 tablespoon Greek yogurt
- 1 egg, beaten
- ¼ cup green olives, sliced
- 1 tablespoon olive oil
- 1/3 cup fresh cilantro, chopped

In the bowl, combine together Mozzarella cheese, spinach, yogurt, egg, olives, and cilantro.
Then pour olive oil in the skillet.
Place one tortilla in the skillet and spread it with Mozzarella mixture. Top it with the second tortilla and spread it with cheese mixture again.
Then place the third tortilla and spread it with all remaining cheese mixture.
Cover it with the last tortilla and fry it for 5 minutes from each side over the medium heat.

**Per serving:** Calories 193, Fat 7.7, Fiber 3.2, Carbs 23.6, Protein 8.3

---

## Creamy Penne

**Prep Time:** 10 min
**Cook Time:** 25 min
**Servings:** 4

- ½ cup penne, dried
- 9 oz chicken fillet
- 1 teaspoon Italian seasoning
- 1 tablespoon olive oil
- 1 tomato, chopped
- 1 cup heavy cream
- 1 tablespoon fresh basil, chopped
- ½ teaspoon salt
- 2 oz Parmesan, grated
- 1 cup water, for cooking

Pour water in the pan, add penne, and boil it for 15 minutes. Then drain water.
Pour olive oil in the skillet and heat it up.
Slice the chicken fillet and put it in the hot oil. Sprinkle chicken with Italian seasoning and roast for 2 minutes from each side.
Then add fresh basil, salt, tomato, and grated cheese.
Stir well.
Add heavy cream and cooked penne.
Cook the meal for 5 minutes more over the medium heat. Stir it from time to time.

**Per serving:** Calories 388, Fat 23.4, Fiber 0.2, Carbs 17.6, Protein 17.6

# Light Paprika Moussaka

**Prep Time:** 15 min
**Cook Time:** 45 min
**Servings:** 3

- 1 eggplant, trimmed
- 1 cup ground chicken
- 1/3 cup white onion, diced
- 3 oz Cheddar cheese, shredded
- 1 potato, sliced
- 1 teaspoon olive oil
- 1 teaspoon salt
- ½ cup milk
- 1 tablespoon butter
- 1 tablespoon ground paprika
- 1 tablespoon Italian seasoning
- 1 teaspoon tomato paste

Slice the eggplant lengthwise and sprinkle with salt.
Pour olive oil in the skillet and add sliced potato.
Roast potato for 2 minutes from each side.
Then transfer it in the plate.
Put eggplant in the skillet and roast it for 2 minutes from each side too.
Pour milk in the pan and bring it to boil.
Add tomato paste, Italian seasoning, paprika, butter, and Cheddar cheese.
Then mix up together onion with ground chicken.
Arrange the sliced potato in the casserole in one layer.
Then add ½ part of all sliced eggplants.
Spread the eggplants with ½ part of chicken mixture.
Then add remaining eggplants.
Pour the milk mixture over the eggplants.
Bake moussaka for 30 minutes at 355F.

**Per serving:** Calories 387, Fat 21.2, Fiber 8.9, Carbs 26.3, Protein 25.4

# Mackerel Skillet with Greens

**Prep Time:** 10 min
**Cook Time:** 15 min
**Servings:** 4

- 1 cup fresh spinach, chopped
- ½ cup endive, chopped
- 11 oz mackerel
- 1 tablespoon olive oil
- 1 teaspoon ground nutmeg
- ½ teaspoon salt
- ½ teaspoon turmeric
- ½ teaspoon chili flakes
- 3 tablespoons sour cream

Pour olive oil in the skillet.
Add mackerel and sprinkle it with chili flakes, turmeric, and salt.
Roast fish for 2 minutes from each side.
Then add chopped endive, fresh spinach, and sour cream.
Mix up well and close the lid.
Simmer the meal for 10 minutes over the medium-low heat.

**Per serving:** Calories 260, Fat 19.5, Fiber 0.5, Carbs 1.3, Protein 19.2

| Dinner

## Zucchini Spaghetti

**Prep Time**: 60-70 min
**Cook Time**: 15 min
**Servings**: 4

- 1/3 cup coconut oil (melted)
- ¼ cup basil (chopped)
- Black pepper to taste
- 2 garlic cloves (minced)
- 4 zucchinis (cut with a spiralizer)
- A pinch of sea salt
- ½ cup walnuts (chopped)

Prepare zucchini spaghetti with a pinch of sea salt and black pepper, set aside for 1 hour, then drain into a bowl. Using medium-high heat, heat up a pan with coconut oil, then add the seasoned zucchini spaghetti and minced garlic, stir and cook for 7 minutes. Pour in the chopped basil and walnuts with black pepper for taste. Stir and cook for 3 minutes longer. Serve the dish as desired.

**Per serving:** Calories 279, Fat 24, Fiber 8, Carbs 11, Protein 6

---

## Dill Carrots

**Prep Time**: 10-20 min
**Cook Time**: 35 min
**Servings**: 4

- 1 tablespoon coconut oil (melted)
- 1-pound baby carrots
- A pinch of black pepper
- 2 tablespoons dill (chopped)
- 1 tablespoon coconut sugar

Boil carrots in a large saucepan using medium-high heat, then allow simmering for 29 minutes covered. Drain carrots into a bowl, add coconut sugar, chopped dill, coconut oil and black pepper to taste, stir properly, then share into dishes and serve.

**Per serving:** Calories 89, Fat 5, Fiber 18, Carbs 14, Protein 3

**Renal Diet Cookbook for Beginners**

## Herbed Vegetable Trout

**Prep Time** 15 min  **Cook Time** 15 min  **Servings** 4

- 14 oz. trout fillets
- 1/2 teaspoon herb seasoning blend
- 1 lemon, sliced
- 2 green onions, sliced
- 1 stalk celery, chopped
- 1 medium carrot, julienne

Prepare and preheat a charcoal grill over moderate heat.
Place the trout fillets over a large piece of foil and drizzle herb seasoning on top.
Spread the lemon slices, carrots, celery, and green onions over the fish.
Cover the fish with foil and pack it.
Place the packed fish in the grill and cook for 15 minutes.
Once done, remove the foil from the fish.
Serve.

**Per serving:** Calories 202, Total Fat 8.5g Saturated Fat 1.5g Cholesterol 73mg Sodium 82mg Carbohydrate 3.5g Dietary Fiber 1.1g Sugars 1.3g Protein 26.9g Calcium 70mg Phosphorous 287mg Potassium 560mg

## Citrus Glazed Salmon

**Prep Time** 15 min  **Cook Time** 20 min  **Servings** 4

- 2 garlic cloves, crushed
- 1 1/2 tablespoons lemon juice
- 2 tablespoons olive oil
- 1 tablespoon butter
- 1 tablespoon Dijon mustard
- 2 dashes cayenne pepper
- 1 teaspoon dried basil leaves
- 1 teaspoon dried dill
- 24 oz. salmon filet

Place a 1-quart saucepan over moderate heat and add the oil, butter, garlic, lemon juice, mustard, cayenne pepper, dill, and basil to the pan.
Stir this mixture for 5 minutes after it has boiled.
Prepare and preheat a charcoal grill over moderate heat.
Place the fish on a foil sheet and fold the edges to make a foil tray.
Pour the prepared sauce over the fish.
Place the fish in the foil in the preheated grill and cook for 12 minutes.
Slice and serve.

**Per serving:** Calories 401, Total Fat 20.5g Saturated Fat 5.3g Cholesterol 144mg Sodium 256mg Carbohydrate 0.5g Dietary Fiber 0.2g Sugars 0.1g Protein 48.4g Calcium 549mg Phosphorous 214mg Potassium 446mg

| Dinner

## Broiled Salmon Fillets

**Prep Time:** 15 min
**Cook Time:** 35 min
**Servings:** 4

- 1 tablespoon ginger root, grated
- 1 clove garlic, minced
- ¼ cup maple syrup
- 1 tablespoon hot pepper sauce
- 4 salmon fillets, skinless

Grease a pan with cooking spray and place it over moderate heat.
Add the ginger and garlic and sauté for 3 minutes then transfer to a bowl.
Add the hot pepper sauce and maple syrup to the ginger-garlic.
Mix well and keep this mixture aside.
Place the salmon fillet in a suitable baking tray, greased with cooking oil.
Brush the maple sauce over the fillets liberally
Broil them for 10 minutes at the oven at broiler settings.
Serve warm.

**Per serving:** Calories 289, Total Fat 11.1g Saturated Fat 1.6g Cholesterol 78mg Sodium 80mg Carbohydrate 13.6g Dietary Fiber 0g Sugars 11.8g Protein 34.6g Calcium 78mg Phosphorous 230mg Potassium 331mg

## Squash and Cranberries

**Prep Time:** 10-15 min
**Cook Time:** 29 min
**Servings:** 2

- 1 tablespoon coconut oil
- 2 garlic cloves (minced)
- 12 ounces of coconut milk
- 1 teaspoon cinnamon powder
- 1 butternut squash (peeled and cubed)
- 1 small yellow onion (chopped)
- 1 teaspoon curry powder
- ½ cup cranberries

Sprinkle cubed squash pieces on a baking sheet, and heat at 400 degrees Fahrenheit for 15 minutes on one side. Using medium-high heat, heat up a pan with coconut oil, then add minced garlic and chopped onion and cook for 5 minutes. Then add the roasted squash stir and allow to cook for 5 minutes longer. Pour in the cranberries, curry powder, cinnamon, coconut milk, stir and allow to cook for 4 minutes longer. The dish is ready.

**Per serving:** Calories 519, Fat 50, Fiber 7, Carbs 24, Protein 7

**Renal Diet Cookbook for Beginners**

## Spicy Sweet Potatoes

**Prep Time** 10-12 min | **Cook Time** 42 min | **Servings** 4

- 4 sweet potatoes (peeled and thinly sliced)
- 2 tablespoon coconut oil (melted)
- Cayenne pepper to taste
- 2 teaspoons nutmeg (ground)

Prepare a mix in a bowl containing sliced sweet potatoes, coconut oil, ground nutmeg and cayenne pepper for taste. Toss to mix well. Spread mixture on a baking sheet and heat at 349 degrees Fahrenheit for 26 minutes. Flip and bake another side for 16 more minutes. Serve as desired.

**Per serving:** Calories 250, Fat 10, Fiber 7, Carbs 50, Protein 5

## Salmon Balls with Cream Cheese

**Prep Time** 15 min | **Cook Time** 15 min | **Servings** 5

- 1-pound salmon fillet
- 2 teaspoons cream cheese
- 3 tablespoons panko breadcrumbs
- ½ teaspoon salt
- 1 oz Parmesan, grated
- ½ teaspoon ground black pepper
- 1 teaspoon dried oregano
- 1 tablespoon sunflower oil

Grind the salmon fillet and combine it together with cream cheese, panko breadcrumbs, salt, Parmesan, ground black pepper, and dried oregano.
Then make the small balls from the mixture and place them in the non-sticky tray.
Sprinkle the balls with sunflower oil and bake in the preheated to the 365F oven for 15 minutes. Flip the balls on another side after 10 minutes of cooking.

**Per serving:** Calories 180, Fat 10.2, Fiber 0.5, Carbs 2.8, Protein 19.9

| Dinner

## Fish Chili with Lentils

**Prep Time:** 10 min
**Cook Time:** 30 min
**Servings:** 4

- 1 red pepper, chopped
- 1 yellow onion, diced
- 1 teaspoon ground black pepper
- 1 teaspoon butter
- 1 jalapeno pepper, chopped
- ½ cup lentils
- 3 cups chicken stock
- 1 teaspoon salt
- 1 tablespoon tomato paste
- 1 teaspoon chili pepper
- 3 tablespoons fresh cilantro, chopped
- 8 oz cod, chopped

Place butter, red pepper, onion, and ground black pepper in the saucepan.
Roast the vegetables for 5 minutes over the medium heat.
Then add chopped jalapeno pepper, lentils, and chili pepper.
Mix up the mixture well and add chicken stock and tomato paste.
Stir until homogenous. Add cod.
Close the lid and cook chili for 20 minutes over the medium heat.

**Per serving:** Calories 187, Fat 2.3, Fiber 8.8, Carbs 21.3, Protein 20.6

## Chili Mussels

**Prep Time:** 7 min
**Cook Time:** 10 min
**Servings:** 4

- 1-pound mussels
- 1 chili pepper, chopped
- 1 cup chicken stock
- ½ cup milk
- 1 teaspoon olive oil
- 1 teaspoon minced garlic
- 1 teaspoon ground coriander
- ½ teaspoon salt
- 1 cup fresh parsley, chopped
- 4 tablespoons lemon juice

Pour milk in the saucepan.
Add chili pepper, chicken stock, olive oil, minced garlic, ground coriander, salt, and lemon juice.
Bring the liquid to boil and add mussels.
Boil the mussel for 4 minutes or until they will open shells.
Then add chopped parsley and mix up the meal well.
Remove it from the heat.

**Per serving:** Calories 136, Fat 4.7, Fiber 0.6, Carbs 7.5, Protein 15.3

## Fried Scallops in Heavy Cream

**Prep Time** 10 min | **Cook Time** 7 min | **Servings** 4

- ½ cup heavy cream
- 1 teaspoon fresh rosemary
- ½ teaspoon dried cumin
- ½ teaspoon garlic, diced
- 8 oz bay scallops
- 1 teaspoon olive oil
- ½ teaspoon salt
- ¼ teaspoon chili flakes

Preheat olive oil in the skillet until hot.
Then sprinkle scallops with salt, chili flakes, and dried cumin and place in the hot oil.
Add fresh rosemary and diced garlic.
Roast the scallops for 2 minutes from each side.
After this, add heavy cream and bring the mixture to boil. Boil it for 1 minute.

**Per serving:** Calories 114, Fat 7.3, Fiber 0.2, Carbs 2.2, Protein 9.9

## Lettuce Seafood Wraps

**Prep Time** 10 min | **Cook Time** 0 min | **Servings** 6

- 6 lettuce leaves
- 8 oz salmon, canned
- 4 oz crab meat, canned
- 1 cucumber
- 2 tablespoons Plain yogurt
- ½ teaspoon minced garlic
- 1 tablespoon fresh dill, chopped
- ¼ teaspoon tarragon

Mash the salmon and crab meat with the help of the fork.
Then add Plain yogurt, minced garlic, fresh dill, and tarragon.
Grate the cucumber and add it in the seafood mixture. Mix up well.
Fill the lettuce leaves with cooked mixture.

**Per serving:** Calories 80, Fat 2.8, Fiber 0.4, Carbs 3.1, Protein 10.5

| Dinner

## Mango Tilapia Fillets

**Prep Time** 10 min | **Cook Time** 15 min | **Servings** 4

- ¼ cup coconut flakes
- 5 oz mango, peeled
- 1/3 cup shallot, chopped
- 1 teaspoon ground turmeric
- 1 cup of water
- 1 bay leaf
- 12 oz tilapia fillets
- 1 chili pepper, chopped
- 1 tablespoon coconut oil
- ½ teaspoon salt
- 1 teaspoon paprika

Blend together coconut flakes, mango, shallot, ground turmeric, and water.
After this, melt coconut oil in the saucepan.
Sprinkle the tilapia fillets with salt and paprika. Then place them in the hot coconut oil and roast for 1 minute from each side.
Add chili pepper, bay leaf, and blended mango mixture.
Close the lid and cook fish for 10 minutes over the medium heat.

**Per serving:** Calories 153, Fat 6.1, Fiber 1.5, Carbs 9.3, Protein 16.8

---

## Seafood Gratin

**Prep Time** 15 min | **Cook Time** 40 min | **Servings** 5

- 3 Russet potatoes, sliced
- ½ cup onion, chopped
- ½ cup milk
- 1 egg, beaten
- 3 tablespoon wheat flour, whole grain
- 1 cup shrimps, peeled
- ½ cup Mozzarella cheese, shredded
- ¼ cup Cheddar cheese, shredded
- 1 teaspoon olive oil
- 1 cup water, for cooking

Pour water in the pan and bring it to boil.
Add sliced potatoes in the hot water and boil it for 3 minutes.
Then remove potatoes from water.
Mix up together beaten egg, milk, chopped onion, flour, and Cheddar cheese.
Preheat the mixture until cheese is melted.
Then place the potatoes in the gratin mold in one layer.
Add the layer of shrimps.
Pour Cheddar cheese mixture over shrimps and top the gratin with Mozzarella cheese.
Cover the gratin with foil and secure the edges.
Bake gratin for 35 minutes at 355F.

**Per serving:** Calories 205, Fat 5.3, Fiber 3.5, Carbs 26.2, Protein 14.1

## Cabbage Beef Borscht

**Prep Time** 15 min  **Cook Time** 25 min  **Servings** 4

- 2 tablespoons vegetable oil
- 3 lbs. beef short ribs
- 1/2 cup dry red wine
- 8 cups low-sodium chicken broth
- 1/2 tablespoon berries
- 1/2 tablespoon whole black peppercorns
- 1/2 tablespoon coriander seeds
- 2 dill sprigs
- 2 oregano sprigs
- 2 parsley sprigs
- 2 tablespoons unsalted butter
- 3 beets (1 1/2 lbs.), peeled and diced
- 1 small rutabaga (1/2 lb.), peeled and diced
- 1 leek, diced
- 1 small onion, diced (1 cup)
- 1/2 lb. carrots, diced
- 2 celery ribs, diced
- 1/2 head savoy cabbage (1 lb.), cored and shredded
- 7 oz. chopped tomatoes, canned
- 1/2 cup dry red wine
- 2 tablespoons red wine vinegar
- Freshly ground pepper
- Sour cream
- Chopped dill
- Horseradish, grated, for serving

Begin by placing the ribs in a large cooking pot and pour enough water to cover it.
Cover the beef pot and cook it on a simmer until it is tender then shred it using a fork.
Add the olive oil, rutabaga, carrots, shredded cabbage, and the remaining ingredients to the cooking liquid in the pot.
Cover the cabbage soup and cook on low heat for 1 ½ hour.
Serve warm.

**Per serving:** Calories 537, Total Fat 45.5g Saturated Fat 19.8g Cholesterol 90mg Sodium 200mg Carbohydrate 10g Dietary Fiber 2.3g Sugars 5.1g Protein 18.7g Calcium 60mg Phosphorous 377mg Potassium 269mg

---

## Lemon Pepper Beef Soup

**Prep Time** 15 min  **Cook Time** 10 min  **Servings** 4

- 1 lb. lean ground beef
- 1/2 cup onion, chopped
- 2 teaspoons lemon-pepper seasoning blend
- 1 cup beef broth
- 2 cups of water
- 1/3 cup white rice, uncooked
- 3 cups of frozen mixed vegetables
- 1 tablespoon sour cream
- Cooking oil

Spray a saucepan with cooking oil and place it over moderate heat.
Toss in the onion and ground beef, and sauté until brown.
Stir in the broth and the rest of the ingredients then boil.
Reduce the heat to a simmer then cover the soup to cook for another 30 minutes.
Garnish with sour cream.
Enjoy.

**Per serving:** Calories 252, Total Fat 5.6g Saturated Fat 2.2g Cholesterol 68mg Sodium 213mg Carbohydrate 21.3g Dietary Fiber 4.3g Sugars 3.4g Protein 27.2g Calcium 42mg Phosphorous 359mg Potassium 211mg

| Dinner

## Cream of Crab Soup

**Prep Time:** 15 min
**Cook Time:** 25 min
**Servings:** 4

- 1 tablespoon unsalted butter
- 1/2 medium onion, chopped
- 1/2 lb. imitation crab meat, shredded
- 1/4 low-sodium chicken broth
- 1 cup coffee creamer
- 2 tablespoons cornstarch
- 1/8 teaspoon dillweed

Add the butter to a cooking pot and melt it over moderate heat.
Toss in the onion and sauté until soft, then stir in the crab meat.
Stir-fry for 3 minutes then add the broth.
Cook up to a boil then reduce the heat to low.
Whisk the coffee creamer with the cornstarch in a bowl until smooth.
Add this cornstarch slurry to the soup and cook until it thickens.
Stir in the dillweed and mix gently.
Serve warm.

**Per serving:** Calories 232, Total Fat 14.7g Saturated Fat 7.8g Cholesterol 51mg Sodium 605mg Carbohydrate 16.7g Dietary Fiber 0.6g Sugars 4.2g Protein 8.1g Calcium 69mg Phosphorous 119mg Potassium 146mg

## Jamaican Drumsticks

**Prep Time:** 15 min
**Cook Time:** 20 min
**Servings:** 4

- 10 chicken drumsticks
- 1/3 cup olive oil
- 2 tablespoons brown Swerve
- 1 tablespoon dried thyme
- 2 teaspoons allspice, ground
- 2 teaspoons smoked paprika
- 1 teaspoon cinnamon
- 1 teaspoon ginger, ground
- 1 teaspoon cloves, ground
- 1 teaspoon cayenne pepper, ground
- 1/4 teaspoon black pepper

Blend everything, except the chicken, in a blender until smooth.
Mix the chicken with the blended mixture in a large Ziplock bag then seal it.
Refrigerate the chicken drumsticks with its marinade for 24 hours.
Prepare and preheat a grill over medium-high heat then grease the grill with cooking spray.
Place the marinated chicken in the grill and grill for 12 minutes per side.
Serve warm.

**Per serving:** Calories 148, Total Fat 9.5g Saturated Fat 1.7g Cholesterol 40mg Sodium 39mg Total Carbohydrate 1.4 g Dietary Fiber 0.6g Sugars 0.4g Protein 13.8g Calcium 19mg Phosphorous 136mg Potassium 120mg

# Chicken with Asparagus

**Prep Time** 15 min    **Cook Time** 15 min    **Servings** 4

- 8 oz. boneless, skinless chicken breast
- 2 1/2 tablespoons olive oil
- 1/2 teaspoon cracked black pepper
- 1/8 teaspoon cumin
- 1/8 teaspoon paprika
- 1/8 teaspoon chili powder
- 1/4 teaspoon crushed red pepper flakes
- 10 asparagus spears
- 1 ear corn on the cob
- 1/2 lemon
- 1 tablespoon chives

Rub the chicken breast with olive oil, herb spice mix, red pepper flakes, and black pepper for seasoning.
Set a suitable grill pan over moderate heat and grill the chicken for 6 minutes per side.
Transfer the chicken to the serving plates.
Now season the asparagus with black pepper and 2 teaspoons of olive oil.
Grill the asparagus for 3 minutes per side then transfer it to the serving plates with the chicken.
Rub the corn ear with 1 teaspoon olive oil and grill for 2 minutes per side.
Transfer the corn ear to the serving plates and add lemon juice and chives on top.
Serve.

**Per serving:** Calories 31, Total Fat 17.4g Saturated Fat 2.1g Cholesterol 73mg Sodium 64mg Carbohydrate 13.8g Dietary Fiber 4.2g Sugars 3.8g Protein 28g Calcium 45mg Phosphorous 239mg Potassium 785mg

# Snacks and Desserts

## Avocado with Walnut Butter Smoothie

**Prep Time** 15 min | **Cook Time** 25 min | **Servings** 4

- 1 avocado (diced)
- 1 cup baby spinach
- 1 cup coconut milk (canned)
- 1 Tbsp walnut butter, unsalted
- 2 Tbsp natural sweetener such as Stevia, Erythritol, Truvia... etc.

Place all Ingredients into food processor or a blender; blend until smooth or to taste.
Add more or less walnut butter.
Drink and enjoy!

**Per serving:** Calories: 364 Carbohydrates: 7g Proteins: 8g Fat: 35g Fiber: 5.5g

## Baby Spinach and Dill Smoothie

**Prep Time** 15 min | **Cook Time** 0 min | **Servings** 4

- 1 cup of fresh baby spinach leaves
- 2 Tbsp of fresh dill, chopped
- 1 1/2 cup of water
- 1/2 avocado, chopped into cubes
- 1 Tbsp chia seeds (optional)
- 2 Tbsp of natural sweetener Stevia or Erythritol (optional)

Place all Ingredients into fast-speed blender. Beat until smooth and all Ingredients united well.
Serve and enjoy!

**Per serving:** Calories: 136 Carbohydrates: 8g Proteins: 7g Fat: 10g Fiber: 9g

**Renal Diet Cookbook for Beginners**

## Blueberries and Coconut Smoothie

**Prep Time**
15 min

**Cook Time**
0 min

**Servings**
4

- 1 cup of frozen blueberries, unsweetened
- 1 cup Stevia or Erythritol sweetener
- 2 cups coconut milk (canned)
- 1 cup of fresh spinach leaves
- 2 Tbsp shredded coconut (unsweetened)
- 3/4 cup water

Place all Ingredients from the list in food-processor or in your strong blender.
Blend for 45 - 60 seconds or to taste.
Ready for drink! Serve!

**Per serving:** Calories: 190 Carbohydrates: 8g Proteins: 3g Fat: 18g Fiber: 2g

## No-Bake Strawberry Cheesecake

**Prep Time**
20 min

**Cook Time**
5 min

**Servings**
8

- **For Crust:**
- 1 cup almonds
- 1 cup pecans
- 2 tablespoons unsweetened coconut flakes
- 6 Medjool dates, pitted, soaked for 10 minutes and drained
- Pinch of salt
- **For Filling:**
- 3 cups cashews, soaked and drained
- ¼ cup organic honey
- ¼ cup fresh lemon juice
- 1/3 cup coconut oil, melted
- 1 teaspoon organic vanilla flavor
- ¼ teaspoon salt
- 1 cup fresh strawberries, hulled and sliced
- **For Topping:**
- 1/3 cup maple syrup
- 1/3 cup water
- Drop of vanilla flavor
- 5 cups fresh strawberries, hulled, sliced and divided

Grease a 9-inch spring foam pan.
For crust in the small mixer, add almonds and pecans and pulse till finely grounded.
Add remaining all ingredients and pulse till smooth.
Transfer the crust mixture into prepared pan, pressing gently downwards. Freeze to create completely.
In a large blender, add all filling ingredients and pulse till creamy and smooth.
Place filling mixture over crust evenly.
Freeze for at least couple of hours or till set completely.
In a pan, add maple syrup, water, vanilla and 1 cup of strawberries on medium-low heat.
Bring to a gentle simmer. Simmer for around 4-5 minutes or till thickens.
Strain the sauce and allow it to go cool completely.
Top the chilled cheesecake with strawberry slices. Drizzle with sauce and serve.

**Per serving:** Calories: 294 Fat: 12g, Carbohydrates: 32g, Fiber: 2g, Protein: 5.2g

Snacks and Desserts

## Raw Lime, Avocado & Coconut Pie

**Prep Time:** 20 min
**Cook Time:** 35 min
**Servings:** 8

- **For Crust:**
- ¾ cup unsweetened coconut flakes
- 1 cup dates, pitted and chopped roughly
- **For Filing:**
- ¾ cup young coconut meat
- 1½ avocados, peeled, pitted and chopped
- 2 tablespoons fresh lime juice
- ¼ cup raw agave nectar

Lightly, grease an 8-inch pie pan.
In a sizable food processor, add all crust ingredients and pulse till smooth.
Transfer the crust mixture into prepared pan, pressing gently downwards.
With a paper towel, wipe out your blender completely.
In the same processor, add all filling ingredients and pulse till smooth.
Place filling mixture over crust evenly.
Freeze not less than 120 minutes or till set completely.

**Per serving:** Calories: 290 Fat: 14g, Carbohydrates: 31g, Fiber: 6g, Protein: 7g

---

## Blackberry & Apple Skillet Cake

**Prep Time:** 20 min
**Cook Time:** 25 min
**Servings:** 4

- **For Filling:**
- 2 tablespoons coconut oil
- 1 tablespoon coconut sugar
- 3 sweet apples, cored and cut into bite sized pieces
- ½ teaspoon ground cinnamon
- ¼ teaspoon ground cardamom
- 1/8 teaspoon ground cloves
- 1/8 teaspoon ground ginger
- 1 cup frozen blackberries
- **For Cake Mixture:**
- ¾ cup ground almonds
- ½ teaspoon baking powder
- 2 tablespoons coconut sugar
- Pinch of salt
- ¼ cup full-Fat coconut milk
- 1 tablespoon coconut oil, melted
- 1 organic egg, beaten
- ½ teaspoon organic vanilla extract

Preheat the oven to 40 degrees F.
In an ovenproof skillet, add butter and coconut sugar on high heat.
Cook, stirring for approximately 2-3 minutes.
Stir in apples and spices and cook, stirring approximately 5 minutes.
Remove from heat and stir in blackberries.
Meanwhile in a bowl, mix together ground almonds, baking powder, coconut sugar and salt.
In another bowl, add remaining ingredients and beat till well combined.
Add egg mixture into ground almond mixture and mix till well combined.
Place a combination over fruit mixture evenly.
Transfer the skillet into oven.
Bake approximately 15-20 min. Serve warm.

**Per serving:** Calories: 294 Fat: 9g, Carbohydrates: 22g, Fiber: 44g, Protein: 6g

Renal Diet Cookbook for Beginners

# Pudding Muffins

**Prep Time** 15 min | **Cook Time** 26 min | **Servings** 5

**For Muffins:**
- 12 dates, pitted and chopped
- 10 tablespoons water
- 2½-3 tablespoons coconut flour
- ½ teaspoon baking powder
- 2 organic eggs
- 1½ bananas, peeled and sliced
- 1 teaspoon organic honey
- 1 tablespoon organic vanilla flavoring

**For Topping:**
- 5-6, pitted and chopped
- 3 tablespoons almond milk
- Fresh juice of ½ orange
- 1 teaspoon organic honey
- 1 teaspoon organic vanilla flavoring

**For Garnishing:**
- Fresh raspberries, as required

Preheat the oven to 365 degrees F. Grease 5 cups of an large muffin tin.
For muffins in a very small pan, mix together dates and water on low heat.
Cook for approximately 3-4 minutes or till the dates break down and be thick.
Remove from heat and having a fork, mash the dates completely.
In a bowl, add remaining ingredients and beat till well combined.
Add mashed dates and stir to combine.
Transfer the mix in prepared muffin cups evenly.
Bake for about 20-22 minutes.
Meanwhile in a pan, add all topping ingredients on low heat.
Cook for about 3-4 minutes or till the dates break up and turn into thick.
Remove from heat and having a fork, mash the dates completely. Keep aside.
Remove muffins from oven and keep aside to cool for approximately 5 minutes.
Carefully, take away the muffins from cups. Top with date mixture evenly.
Garnish with raspberries and serve

**Per serving:** Calories: 287 Fat: 7g, Carbohydrates: 27g, Fiber: 6g, Protein: 9 g

# Black Forest Pudding

**Prep Time** 15 min | **Cook Time** 2 min | **Servings** 2

- 1 teaspoon coconut cream
- 1 teaspoon coconut oil
- 3-4 squares 70% chocolate bars, chopped
- 1 cup coconut cream, whipped till thick and divided
- 2 cups fresh cherries, pitted and quartered
- 70% chocolate bars shaving, for garnishing
- Shredded coconut, for garnishing

In a smaller pan, add 1 teaspoon coconut cream, coconut oil and chopped chocolate on low heat.
Cook, stirring continuously for about 2 minutes or till thick and glossy. Immediately, remove from heat.
In 2 serving glasses, divide chocolate sauce evenly.
Now, place ½ cup of cream over chocolate sauce in the glasses.
Divide cherries in glasses evenly.
Top with remaining coconut cream.
Garnish with chocolate shaving and shredded coconut.

**Per serving:** Calories: 302 Fat: 10g, Carbohydrates: 30g, Fiber: 3g, Protein: 4g

| Snacks and Desserts

## Pineapple Sticks

**Prep Time** 15 min  **Cook Time** 20 min  **Servings** 2

- ¼ cup fresh orange juice
- ¾ cup coconut, shredded an d toasted
- 8 (3x1-inch) fresh pineapple pieces

Line a baking sheet with wax paper.
In a shallow dish, place pineapple juice.
In another shallow dish, squeeze pineapple.
Insert 1 wooden skewer in each pineapple piece through the narrow end.
Dip each pineapple piece in juice and then coat with coconut evenly.
Arrange the pineapple sticks onto prepared baking sheet inside a single layer.
Cover and freeze for around 1-2 hours.

**Per serving:** Calories: 65, Fat: 3g, Carbohydrates: 10g, Fiber: 1g, Protein: 0g

## Fried Pineapple Slices

**Prep Time** 15 min  **Cook Time** 6 min  **Servings** 6-8

- 1 fresh pineapple, peeled and cut into large slices
- ¼ cup coconut oil
- ¼ cup coconut palm sugar
- ¼ teaspoon ground cinnamon

Heat a large surefire skillet on medium heat.
Stir in oil and sugar till coconut oil is very melted.
Add pineapple slices in batches and cook for approximately 1-2 minutes.
Carefully flip the side and cook for around 1 minute.
Cook for approximately 1 minute more.
Repeat with remaining slices.
Sprinkle with cinnamon and serve.

**Per serving:** Calories: 97 Fat: 1g, Carbohydrates: 12g, Fiber: 2g, Protein: 1g

## Grilled Peaches

**Prep Time:** 15 min
**Cook Time:** 10 min
**Servings:** 6

- 3 medium peaches, halved and pitted
- ½ cup coconut cream
- 1 teaspoon vanilla flavoring
- ¼ cup walnuts, chopped
- Ground cinnamon, as required

Preheat the grill to medium-low heat. Grease the grill grate.
Arrange the peach slices onto grill, cut side down.
Grill for approximately 3-5 minutes per side or till desired doneness.
Meanwhile inside a bowl, add coconut cream and vanilla extract and beat till smooth.
Spoon the whipped cream over each peach half.
Top with walnuts and sprinkle with cinnamon and serve.

**Per serving:** Calories: 286 Fat: 7g, Carbohydrates: 22g, Fiber: 4g, Protein: 8g

## Baked Apples

**Prep Time:** 15 min
**Cook Time:** 18 min
**Servings:** 4

- 4 tart apples, cored
- ¼ cup coconut oil, softened
- 4 teaspoons ground cinnamon
- 1/8 teaspoon ground ginger
- 1/8 teaspoon ground nutmeg

Preheat the oven to 350 degrees F.
Fill each apple with 1 tablespoon of coconut oil.
Sprinkle with spices evenly.
Arrange the apples onto a baking sheet.
Bake for around 12-18 minutes.

**Per serving:** Calories: 285 Fat: 8g, Carbohydrates: 17g, Fiber: 3g, Protein: 52g

| Snacks and Desserts

## Stuffed Apples

**Prep Time:** 15 min
**Cook Time:** 35 min
**Servings:** 4

- 4 large apples, peeled and cored
- 2 teaspoons fresh lemon juice
- 1 cup fresh blueberries
- ½ cup fresh apple juice
- ½ teaspoon ground cinnamon
- ¼ cup almond meal
- ¼ cup coconut flakes

Preheat the oven to 375 degrees F.
Coat the apples with lemon juice evenly.
Arrange the apples inside a baking dish.
Stuff each apple with blueberries.
Scatter the rest of the blueberries around the apples.
Drizzle with apple juice.
Sprinkle each apple with cinnamon evenly.
Top with almond meal and coconut flakes evenly.
Bake approximately 30-35 minutes.

**Per serving:** Calories: 200, Fat: 2g, Carbohydrates: 15g, Fiber: 1g, Protein: 4g

## Rhubarb & Blueberry Granita

**Prep Time:** 15 min
**Cook Time:** 10 min
**Servings:** 8

- 1 cup fresh blueberries
- 3 cups rhubarb, sliced
- ½ cup raw honey
- 2½ cups water
- Fresh mint leaves, for garnishing

In a pan, add all ingredients on medium heat.
Cook, stirring occasionally for around 10 minutes.
Strain the mix through a strainer by pressing a combination.
Discard the pulp of fruit.
Transfer the strained mixture right into a 13x9-inch glass baking dish.
Freeze for around 20-a half-hour.
Remove from freezer and with a fork scrap the mix.
Cover and freeze for approximately 60 minutes, scraping after every half an hour.

**Per serving:** Calories: 122, Fat: 2g, Carbohydrates: 16g, Fiber: 2g, Protein: 6.1g

## Citrus Strawberry Granita

**Prep Time:** 15 min
**Cook Time:** 5 min
**Servings:** 4

- 12-ounce fresh strawberries. Hulled
- 1 grapefruit, peeled, seeded and sectioned
- 2 oranges, peeled, seeded and sectioned
- ¼ of a lemon
- ¼ cup raw honey

In a juicer add strawberries, grapefruit, oranges and lemon and process based on manufacturer's directions.
In a pan, add 1½ cups from the fruit juice and honey on medium heat.
Cook, stirring approximately 5 minutes.
Remove from heat and stir within the remaining juice.
Keep aside to cool for approximately a half-hour.
Transfer the juice mixture into an 8x8-inch glass baking dish.
Freeze for approximately 4 hours, scraping after every 30 minutes.

**Per serving:** Calories: 211, Fat: 2g, Carbohydrates: 19g, Fiber: 3g, Protein: 2g

## Pumpkin Ice-Cream

**Prep Time:** 15 min
**Cook Time:** 50 min
**Servings:** 4

- 1 (15-ounce) can pumpkin puree
- ½ cup dates, pitted and chopped
- 2 (14-ounce) cans coconut milk
- ½ teaspoon vanilla extract
- 1½ teaspoons pumpkin pie spice
- ½ teaspoon ground cinnamon
- Pinch of salt

In an increased speed blender, add all ingredients and pulse till smooth.
Transfer into an airtight container and freeze for approximately 1-couple of hours.
Now, transfer into an ice-cream maker and process based on manufacturer's directions.
Return the ice-cream into airtight container and freeze for approximately 1-couple of hours.

**Per serving:** Calories: 103, Fat: 6g, Carbohydrates: 16g, Fiber: 5g, Protein: 7g

| Snacks and Desserts

# Chocolaty Cherry Ice-Cream

**Prep Time** 15 min
**Cook Time** 5 min
**Servings** 4

- 1 cup raw cashews
- 1 cup frozen cherries
- ¼ cup coconut, shredded
- 1 tablespoon raw honey
- ¼ cup chocolate bars, chopped

In a higher speed blender, add cashews and pulse till a flour like texture forms.
Add remaining ingredients except chocolate and pulse till smooth.
Add chocolate and pulse till just combined. Transfer the ice-cream into airtight container and freeze for about 1-120 minutes or till set.

**Per serving:** Calories: 135, Fat: 9g, Carbohydrates: 23g, Fiber: 4g, Protein: 12g

# Collard Greens and Cucumber Smoothie

**Prep Time** 15 min
**Cook Time** 0 min
**Servings** 4

- 1 cup Collard greens
- A few fresh pepper mint leaves
- 1 big cucumber
- 1 lime, freshly juiced
- 1/2 cups avocado sliced
- 1 1/2 cup water
- 1 cup crushed ice
- 1/4 cup of natural sweetener Erythritol or Stevia (optional)

Rinse and clean your Collard greens from any dirt.
Place all Ingredients in a food processor or blender,
Blend until all Ingredients in your smoothie is combined well.
Pour in a glass and drink. Enjoy!

**Per serving:** Calories: 123 Carbohydrates: 8g Proteins: 4g Fat: 11g Fiber: 6g

Renal Diet Cookbook for Beginners

## Creamy Dandelion Greens and Celery Smoothie

**Prep Time** 15 min    **Cook Time** 0 min    **Servings** 4

- 1 handful of raw dandelion greens
- 2 celery sticks
- 2 Tbsp chia seeds
- 1 small piece of ginger, minced
- 1/2 cup almond milk
- 1/2 cup of water
- 1/2 cup plain yogurt

Rinse and clean dandelion leaves from any dirt; add in a high-speed blender.
Clean the ginger; keep only inner part and cut in small slices; add in a blender.
Add all remaining Ingredients and blend until smooth.
Serve and enjoy!

**Per serving:** Calories: 58 Carbohydrates: 5g Proteins: 3g Fat: 6g Fiber: 3g

## Dark Turnip Greens Smoothie

**Prep Time** 15 min    **Cook Time** 0 min    **Servings** 4

- 1 cup of raw turnip greens
- 1 1/2 cup of almond milk
- 1 Tbsp of almond butter
- 1/2 cup of water
- 1/2 tsp of cocoa powder, unsweetened
- 1 Tbsp of dark chocolate chips
- 1/4 tsp of cinnamon
- A pinch of salt
- 1/2 cup of crushed ice

Rinse and clean turnip greens from any dirt.
Place the turnip greens in your blender along with all other Ingredients.
Blend it for 45 - 60 seconds or until done; smooth and creamy.
Serve with or without crushed ice.

**Per serving:** Calories: 131 Carbohydrates: 6g Proteins: 4g Fat: 10g Fiber: 2.5g

| Snacks and Desserts

# Butter Pecan and Coconut Smoothie

**Prep Time** 15 min | **Cook Time** 0 min | **Servings** 4

- 1 cup coconut milk, canned
- 1 scoop Butter Pecan powdered cream er
- 2 cups fresh spinach leaves, chopped
- 1/2 banana frozen or fresh
- 2 Tbsp stevia granulated sweetener to taste
- 1/2 cup water
- 1 cup ice cubes crushed

Place Ingredients from the list above in your high-speed blender.
Blend for 35 - 50 seconds or until all Ingredients combined well.
Add less or more crushed ice.
Drink and enjoy!

**Per serving:** Calories: 268 Carbohydrates: 7g Proteins: 6g Fat: 26g Fiber: 1.5g

# Fresh Cucumber, Kale and Raspberry Smoothie

**Prep Time** 15 min | **Cook Time** 0 min | **Servings** 4

- 1 1/2 cups of cucumber, peeled
- 1/2 cup raw kale leaves
- 1 1/2 cups fresh raspberries
- 1 cup of almond milk
- 1 cup of water
- Ice cubes crushed (optional)
- 2 Tbsp natural sweetener (Stevia, Erythritol... etc.)

Place all Ingredients from the list in a food processor or high-speed blender; blend for 35 - 40 seconds.
Serve into chilled glasses.
Add more natural sweeter if you like. Enjoy!

**Per serving:** Calories: 70 Carbohydrates: 8g Proteins: 3g Fat: 6g Fiber: 5g

Renal Diet Cookbook for Beginners | 77

## Almond Truffles

**Prep Time:** 15 min
**Cook Time:** 20 min
**Servings:** 4

- ½ cup almond flour
- 1 tablespoon heavy cream
- ¾ teaspoon cinnamon (ground)
- 1 oz dark chocolate
- 2 teaspoons almond butter
- 1 teaspoon liquid stevia

Prepare a mix containing the almond butter with flour, then add in the liquid stevia with grounded cinnamon and mix thoroughly till smooth. Mold about 5 truffles, place on parchment, and free for 13 minutes. Preheat the heavy cream and dark chocolate to an even mixture. Bring in almond truffles and sprinkle with the mixe chocolate spread. Allow the frozen truffles in room temperature for a while. Serve as desired!

**Per serving:** Calories 100, Fat 8, Fiber 3, Carbs 9, Protein 5

## Banana Foster Pie

**Prep Time:** 15 min
**Cook Time:** 20 min
**Servings:** 4

- ¼ cup granulated sugar
- 1 teaspoon baking soda
- 2 large eggs
- 2 teaspoon pure vanilla extract
- 1 cup peanut butter (unsalted)
- 2 cups all-purpose flour
- 2 tablespoons butter
- 4 ounces softened cream cheese

Prepare a mix with consistent whipping containing coconut cream, arrowroot, cashew butter, nutmeg, coconut sugar and cinnamon for 3 minutes. Pour in the melted coconut oil, rum and vanilla, then allow refrigerate the mixture for 28 minutes. Top the mixture with sugar to get a brown banana coloration and mix with rum (¼ teaspoon). Heat up using medium heat but allow to cook for 4 minutes. Layer the pie crust on the banana and spread chilled cream on it. Allow to chill for 5 hours 30 minutes and sprinkle with toppings (Coconut sugar). Enjoy your dessert!

**Per serving:** Calories 600, Fat 50, Fiber 6, Carbs 53, Protein 8

| Snacks and Desserts

# Fresh Lettuce and Cucumber-Lemon Smoothie

**Prep Time**
15 min

**Cook Time**
0 min

**Servings**
4

- 2 cups fresh lettuce leaves, chopped (any kind)
- 1 cup of cucumber
- 1 lemon washed and sliced.
- 1/2 avocado
- 2 Tbsp chia seeds
- 1 1/2 cup water or coconut water
- 1/4 cup stevia granulate sweetener (or to taste)

Add all Ingredients from the list above in the high-speed blender; blend until completely smooth.
Pour your smoothie into chilled glasses and enjoy!

**Per serving:** Calories: 51 Carbohydrates: 4g Proteins: 2g Fat: 4g Fiber: 3.5g

# Conclusion

Thank you for making it to the end of this book. You have learned what chronic kidney disease is and what the stages are. You now know what your body is going through and the causes. These are just your first steps in working through your diagnosis, or the diagnosis of someone that you love. Because this is a lifestyle change, you will constantly be learning new things and how to help yourself live the best life possible. There are no guarantees that a cure will be found for chronic kidney disease in the near future, but you can start making the first step to avoiding dialysis. Catching the disease early is important, and even if you only fear you may be developing CKD, these tips will help you thwart the progression.

Even with a disease that limits so many foods, you can still make delicious treats and meals by the alternatives provided. You can also customize them according to your palate so that the food you eat not only helps your body but also boosts your mood. You can share these tasty renal-friendly meals with your friends and family and live a long life with them by your side!

As you live your life experiencing each wonderful dish in this book, know that you are living one more wonderful moment. And sometimes, that is all that is required. One more wonderful moment. Renal diet may seem restricting for many, but in reality, there is plenty of low sodium, low phosphorus, and low potassium options to try out and we have proven it with this recipe book.

Keep in mind that we have included roughly the levels of all these minerals in every recipe separately and therefore, you will have to calculate the total amounts you consume each day with all your daily meals.

Living a kidney-friendly life doesn't mean that you are taking away all of the foods that you love; it just means that you may have to be more diligent in the moderation of your food or fluid intake. When your kidneys are not functioning as they should be, it can cause strain on the other organs your body depends on to function. That is why early diagnosis is important with chronic kidney disease so that you can be a key player in slowing the progression of the disease by changing your lifestyle.

The resources included are not intended to replace your doctor or a renal dietician, but to give you options for food choices and seasoning alternatives. Make sure that you are keeping a journal of the foods you are eating and the ones you intend on trying so that your doctor or dietician can help you make an informed decision on whether the diet plan you are trying will work for your stage and severity of kidney disease.

If your kidneys are healthy and happy, the rest of your body is healthy and happy as well because it does not have to overwork itself or put unnecessary strain on other organs.

Don't forget to do regular doctor check-ups to monitor your progress. Be more positive. Live with more hope. Eat with more delight.

## Index of Recipes

**A**
Almond Truffles    78
Apple Muesli  40
Artichoke Matzo Mina    54
Avocado with Walnut Butter Smoothie    67

**B**
Baby Spinach and Dill Smoothie    67
Baked Apples  72
Baked Meatballs & Scallions  44
Banana Foster Pie    78
Basil Zucchini Spaghetti    45
Black Forest Pudding  70
Blackberry & Apple Skillet Cake    69
Blueberries and Coconut Smoothie    68
Bok Choy And Beets  51
Braised Cabbage    46
Breakfast Casserole    32
Breakfast Crepes    33
Broiled Salmon Fillets 59
Buckwheat Granola    31
Butter Pecan and Coconut Smoothie  77

**C**
Cabbage Beef Borscht 64
Carrot Casserole    50
Cauliflower and Leeks    46
Cauliflower Rice    51
Celery and Kale Mix    49
Chia Pudding  29
Chicken Chili  47
Chicken Leftovers Chowder    43
Chicken with Asparagus    66
Chili Mussels  61
Chili Veggie and Quinoa Bowl    37
Chocolaty Cherry Ice-Cream  75
Citrus Glazed Salmon 58
Citrus Strawberry Granita    74
Collard Greens and Cucumber Smoothie
Cream of Crab Soup  65
Creamy Dandelion Greens and Celery Smoothie 76
Creamy Penne    55

**D**
Dark Turnip Greens Smoothie    76
Dill Carrots    57
Duck with Bok Choy  41

**E**
Egg Pockets    32
Eggplant and Mushroom Sauté    47

**F**
Fish Chili with Lentils    61
Fresh Cucumber, Kale and Raspberry Smoothie 77
Fresh Lettuce and Cucumber-Lemon Smoothie 79
Fried Pineapple Slices 71
Fried Scallops in Heavy Cream    62

**G**
Ginger Cauliflower Rice    45
Goat Cheese Omelet  29
Greek Style Quesadillas    55
Grilled Duck Breast & Peach  41
Grilled Peaches    72

**H**
Herbed Vegetable Trout    58

**I**
Italian Eggs with Peppers    33

**J**
Jamaican Drumsticks  65

**K**
Kale Smoothie    39
Kale, Mushrooms and Red Chard Mix    50
Kidney friendly Porridge    35

**L**
Lamb & Pineapple Kebabs    43
Lamb Stew    48
Lemon Pepper Beef Soup    64
Lettuce Seafood Wraps    62
Light Paprika Moussaka    56

**M**
Mackerel Skillet with Greens  56
Mango Tilapia Fillets 63
Millet Muffins 39
Mint Zucchini    49
Mushroom Frittata    31

**N**
No-Bake Strawberry Cheesecake    68

**P**
Pineapple Sticks    71
Pork with Bell Pepper 52
Pork with Pineapple    52
Pudding Muffins    70
Pumpkin Ice-Cream    74

**R**
Raw Lime, Avocado & Coconut Pie    69
Rhubarb & Blueberry Granita    73
Rhubarb Muffins    30
Rosemary Oats    38

**S**
Salmon Balls with Cream Cheese   60
Sausage & Egg Soup   48
Seafood Gratin   63
Slow Cooker Turkey Legs   42
Spiced Pork   53
Spicy Sweet Potatoes   60
Squash and Cranberries   59
Strawberry Muesli   28
Stuffed Apples   73
Stuffed Artichokes   44
Stuffed Zucchini Boats with Goat Cheese
Swiss Chard Bowls   38

**T**
Turkey and Cauliflower Soup   42

**V**
Veggie Bowls   37
Veggie Mix of Mediterranean   36
Veggies Mix of Colors   36

**W**
Winter Berry Smoothie   34
Winter Fruit Salad   30

**Y**
Yogurt Bulgur   28

**Z**
Zucchini and Egg Bowl   35
Zucchini Fritters With Garlic Sauce   34
Zucchini Spaghetti   57

Made in the USA
Las Vegas, NV
05 November 2022